Manifesto of the Free Humans
Part 3 of The Conscious Resistance Trilogy
By John Vibes and Derrick Broze

Cover art by Neil C. Radimaker – Edited by Chris James

Manifesto of the Free Humans
By John Vibes & Derrick Broze

Note from Derrick and John

Thank you for taking the time to conclude the journey that we began in 2015 with the release of *Reflections on Anarchy and Spirituality*. By examining the intersection of spiritual practices predating organized religion and the political philosophy known as Anarchism, we believe we successfully carved out a new path for those who reject authority in their spiritual and political beliefs. *Reflections* laid the foundation for what we believe can help create a more balanced, and free world. It could be considered the "body" of our philosophy.

The second book, *Finding Freedom In An Age of Confusion,* could also be considered the "heart" of our ideas. In a series of essays we explored the human struggle for freedom. We talked about how to overcome the depression, confusion, and fear that often comes along with understanding the harsh realities of our world. For this final installment in our series, we will explore various corners of anarchist philosophy and provide workable solutions for creating a free society. This book could be considered the "mind" of our philosophy. Our goal is to provide our brothers and sisters with a "how to" guide for individual healing and empowerment, community building, and ultimately, for breaking away from the State to form new communities.

In *Reflections* we briefly explored the history of the anarchist philosophy and the American libertarian movement. By providing the history of the thinkers and ideas we are drawing from we hoped to illustrate the evolution of the concepts that have come to be known as The Conscious Resistance. Our focus has been the libertarian and anarchist movements because they have historically contained the most radical activism and propaganda. Although the term "libertarian" may have varied meanings around the world, it is a term that is rooted in an anti-authoritarian, anti-statist philosophy. In America, this libertarian philosophy can be traced back to Josiah Warren, America's first individualist anarchist.

Warren was born in the late 18th century and helped expound the doctrine of individualist anarchism. He was responsible for launching several intentional communities (Utopia, Ohio; Modern Times, NY) that operated under his "Sovereignty of the Individual" ethic, which we explore in the 3rd part of this book. Warren would go on to work with and inspire Lysander Spooner, Benjamin Tucker, Voltairine de Cleyre, and other American Anarchists, many of whom became known as The Boston Anarchists. (For more information we recommend reading *Men Against The State*) The work of these men and women would influence Austrian economist Murray Rothbard and other young freedom minded Americans during the 1960's. Rothbard would borrow ideas and inspiration from the Boston Anarchists, and add Austrian economics and subjective value theory to craft his philosophy of Anarcho-Capitalism. We perceive our work as a continuation and expansion of the Individualist Anarchist tradition that predates the many modern Anarchist divisions, such as Anarcho-Communism and Anarcho-Capitalism. We also hope to expand upon and continue Samuel Konkin's Agorist philosophy.

Readers should note that use of the term "libertarian" refers to the philosophy that includes self-ownership, anti-authoritarianism, and individual sovereignty, not the American Libertarian Party, which we see as contradictory to libertarian and anarchist values. We do not intend to propose a one size fits all model of anarchism, but instead seek to establish a world where people are free to move in and out of competing economic and political systems. This is commonly referred to as "panarchy" or "panarchism," a concept that we will explore in depth later in the book. This would allow individuals the freedom to vacate the state in favor of self-governance, or, if they choose, stay under the rule of the unsustainable state. However, we believe the inevitable and ongoing consciousness shift will erase the notion that statism and authoritarianism has any place in our world. We believe this shift in values and perceptions will lead to a lack of demand for continuing to live under the rule of government.

Finally, please do not forget that each of you are powerful, beautiful, and free. The future depends entirely on the actions we choose to take today. We hope the following essays provide inspiration for those seeking to join the fight for a more free world.

Part 1: A Strategy for Defeating the State

Overcoming the Fear of Freedom

Anarchy! It might be the most feared and propagandized term in existence. The public has an extremely distorted perception of the word and most seem to be terrified of removing authority from their lives and allowing for self-organization. In fact, it is actually extremely rare for serious discussions on this topic to happen due to the knee jerk reactions that are provoked when individuals are presented with the possibility of a world without authority. However, once one is able to find the courage to step beyond social convention and question the control systems they were born into, they will find that real anarchy is actually nothing like the doomsday fiction presented by mainstream culture.

When looking deep enough into this situation it becomes clear that the serious problems facing our species, such as war, poverty, and environmental destruction, are all exacerbated, if not created, by the legalized monopoly on force made possible by government. Ironically, these problems are always cited as reasons to keep the state intact, when in reality, it is the state that is creating the problems in the first place. For centuries, those who reap benefits from the concept of authority have worked tirelessly to keep this idea alive. The parasite class has fought against the rising tide of human ingenuity which has been progressively tearing away from the destructive traditions and control mechanisms of the past. Unfortunately, every time humanity has managed to overcome one oppressive tradition, the ruling class has been able to modify their propaganda to form a more convincing case for their authority.

In the case of racial slavery in the American south, many slaves who were bred into a life of servitude actually held the belief that slavery was not only a necessary price to pay for "civilization" but was also in their best interest. When reading *"The Narrative of the Life of Frederick Douglass,"* one cannot help but notice the similarities between the brainwashing of colonial American slaves and the entranced modern American public. In his autobiography, Douglass points out that slaves would often argue about who had the better and wealthier master. He also described how many slaves came to equate slavery with wealth, and many slaves, Douglass included, believed that in the absence of slavery there would be no wealth, much in the same way that citizens today believe that there would be no peace or prosperity without government. The book details how Douglass had to first remove the chains of mental slavery before he could escape his physical bondage. One of the most profound passages describes the moment when he finally saw the north first hand and learned that wealth could be achieved without slavery.

Douglass wrote that, "*I had very strangely supposed, while in slavery, that few of the comforts, and scarcely any of the luxuries, of life were enjoyed at the north, compared with what were enjoyed by the slaveholders of the south. I probably came to this conclusion from the fact that northern people owned no slaves. I supposed that they were about upon a level with the non-slaveholding population of the south. I knew they were exceedingly poor, and I had been accustomed to regard their poverty as the necessary consequence of their being non-slaveholders. I had somehow imbibed the opinion that, in the absence of slaves, there could be no wealth, and very little refinement. And upon coming to the north, I expected to meet with a rough, hard-handed, and uncultivated population, living in the most Spartan-like simplicity, knowing nothing of the ease, luxury, pomp, and grandeur of southern slaveholders. Such being my conjectures, any one acquainted with the appearance of New Bedford may very readily infer how palpably I must have seen my mistake.*"

In humanity's dark history there were periods where gangs of men could own the lives of millions by claiming to be given that right by a supernatural being. Once that excuse fell out of favor, the power hungry authoritarians were forced to create new justifications for their authority. This desire for elite groups of individuals to rule over large areas of land and conquer the inhabitants within is what gave rise to our current political paradigm. The popular myth states that "the people" created things like governments and militaries as a compromise, to create a mostly peaceful world. In reality, these organizations were all created by sophists and aristocrats, specifically intending to enslave entire populations. As the general public has become more intelligent, increasingly complex rationalizations for authoritarian powers have become necessary to keep the herds in line.

Ideas like the social contract, the national interest, common good, majority rule and representative government have replaced the divine right of kings and the privilege of the aristocracy. In today's more sophisticated culture it is necessary to make people believe they rule themselves in order to effectively rule over them. This is why the rhetoric of the social control systems that we live under is riddled with euphemisms that hide the oppressive and violent nature of their existence. The mass murder of innocent people is called defense, strong arm robbery is called taxation, kidnap and extortion is called justice and gangs of people who claim dominion over specific geographic locations are called governments.

"Government" is itself another one of the words that mean different things to different people, but when examined objectively, it becomes apparent that organizations known as government always maintain a monopoly on the use of force over a given territory. Considering that this is the primary characteristic shared by all governments throughout history, to describe the entity as anything other than a monopoly of violence is euphemistic and dishonest.

We are surrounded by a false definition of the word "government" just as we are surrounded by a false definition of the word "anarchy". We have been told that the word "government" is simply the inevitable form civilized society takes, but this may be one of the most deceptive linguistic tricks used since the dark ages, as it implies that structure and organization will cease to exist in the absence of institutionalized violence and central planners. Since all governments share the common characteristic of establishing and promoting institutionalized violence, we can safely say that a lack of government would increase the opportunity for peace. In other words, when there is peaceful, spontaneous order in a society, there is anarchy, but when a society is organized around the constant threat of institutionalized violence, there is government. This is not to say that violence would never occur in a society without government, but it would not be justified and celebrated, nor would it be as widespread or powerful.

Despite the obvious violence inherent in the institution of government, many people have a difficult time considering the possibility of a world without such a monopoly. When someone suggests that we simply do away with this unjust and unnecessary organization they are typically met with negative reactions. This conversation often ends very quickly because both sides have completely different ideas of what the word "government" actually means. If we attempt to examine government from an outsider's perspective, we would see a world where people are grouped into two different categories - those in government and those not. At face value we can see that these two groups of people have completely different standards and expectations, even though they are the same species and have the same basic needs. Looking closer, we can see that these different standards and laws are not neutral, and in fact, they are very much benefiting those in government at the expense of those who are not. The most important discrepancy to mention here is the fact that many government employees and agents of the state have the "legal" authority to steal, cage, or kill you.

However, if you ask any random person on the street to define "government" for you they will likely repeat the propaganda taught in government school. You know, the tale about how government is the backbone of civilization and the means by which people in the community come together for mutually beneficial projects. This may sound good, but it isn't at all true, because the government does not produce anything and would not be able to provide any "services" if it wasn't for the resources forcibly extracted from the rest of society. Therefore, it is safe to say that all functions that are currently being carried out by the organization known as "government" could actually be better served by individuals in the community working together for common goals, without the middleman, since all the resources and labor is coming from them to begin with. Voluntary trade, charity, and other peaceful methods of interacting would create a far better society than the one that we see today.

The most common argument against having a stateless society is the notion that we are all stupid, worthless savages who would not be able to figure out how to build something as simple as a road if there wasn't someone with a gun in our face every step of the way, telling us how, when, and where to do it. But if people are stupid savages, and politicians are people, then isn't the government made up of a bunch of stupid savages who should not be trusted with a license to kill? If we are all equal and supposedly incapable of governing ourselves, why should we trust other incompetent people to rule over us?

Of course, we know this to be propaganda spread by the powers that wish they were. There is nothing that a government can do that you and a large group of focused individuals cannot also accomplish. The government doesn't provide services, they simply take money from everyone and use a small portion to sell back "services" to the people. Looked at in these terms, it becomes apparent that the government is nothing more than a violent middleman who forces their way into nearly every interaction that takes place between each of its so-called "citizens." Everything that the government does is an attack on people who don't belong to that organization.

If you think about it, every single action the government takes is some kind of punitive measure against people who are not part of the club. Even when the government claims to do something for the goodwill of all people, they are doing so with resources collected by using threats and violence. There is no such thing as a virtuous act of government. This organization is not here to protect our rights. In fact, when the government steps in and gives itself the responsibility to protect your rights, it is simultaneously stripping you of your ability to defend yourself. When you are dependent upon the whims and capabilities of another human being to protect your rights, you are literally handing your rights over to them and opening yourself to slavery.

Although there are only a few examples of stateless societies and communities throughout history that we know of, this should not be seen as a failure of anarchist philosophy. The lack of examples says more about the primitive condition of the human race thus far, than it does about the possibility of a stateless society. Humanity is constantly accomplishing feats and smashing paradigms previously believed to be impossible. So to say that a society without institutionalized violence is impossible because there are not many historical examples, is to say that our current state of affairs is the pinnacle of human achievement. This is obviously a naive, arrogant and blatantly false worldview, which has been projected onto the entire planet through the institutions and conventions established by those who claim ownership over other free human beings.

These institutions and conventions are the very reason why many people have such a distorted view of words like "government" and "anarchy". Our cultural norms have been handed down from those in power, so it is only natural that these norms reflect the needs and interests of the power structure rather than the needs of the people. Therefore, the perceptions of government and anarchy that many of us have adopted are not accurate descriptions of reality, but simply a description of the world as seen through the eyes of our rulers. In a system of government our rulers have infinite power and control. In the absence of government they are forced to live by the same rules and standards as everyone else. The ill-informed will make the mistake of believing that anarchy means without rules, but what it truly means is without centralized authority ruling over others.

In the eyes of a tyrant, a world without complete dominion over the lives of others is a life of lawlessness, chaos, and disorder. This view does not reflect reality, but instead reflects the deranged worldview that drives the parasitic State and corporate classes. This is why a peaceful term like anarchy has such a negative social stigma, while a word like government is seen as a benign and unquestionable construct of nature. We have adopted the language and worldview of our oppressors. It's time for the free hearts and minds of the world to overcome the fear of freedom, reject the authoritarians and statists, and begin governing ourselves.

What is Agorism?

In the late 1970's, anarchist, activist, and writer Samuel E. Konkin III (SEKIII) released *The New Libertarian Manifesto*, presenting his case for a new strain of libertarianism that he called "New Libertarianism". The philosophy behind the New Libertarian Movement was agorism, named after the "agora", the Greek word for marketplace. *"An agorist is one who acts consistently for freedom and in freedom,"* SEKIII wrote.

Essentially, agorism is a radical libertarian philosophy that seeks to create a society free of coercion and force by using black and gray markets in the underground or "illegal" economy to siphon power away from the state. Konkin termed this strategy "counter-economics", which he considered to be all peaceful economic activity that takes place outside the purview and control of the state. This includes competing currencies, community gardening schemes, tax resistance and operating a business without licenses. Agorism also extends to the creation of alternative education programs, free schools or skill shares, and independent media ventures that counter the establishment narratives. Also essential to the growth of agorism is the public's support of entrepreneurs who actively do business outside of the state's license and regulations.

In the NLM, SEKIII outlines his vision of a more free and just world by first describing society's present condition: statism. Konkin briefly outlines the path of human thinking from slavery to the discovery of libertarian thought and also emphasizes the importance of consistency between means and ends. Indeed, Konkin believes exposing statist inconsistencies is *"the most crucial activity of the libertarian theorist."* From here Konkin describes the goal of agorism and the counter economic means necessary to achieve this goal.

In order to paint a clear picture of the agorist struggle for a more free world, Konkin explains the four stages from statism to agorism, as well as various actions that a consciously practicing agorist might seize upon in order to advance agorist propaganda and counter-economic activity. By understanding Konkin's vision of progress, it is possible to create a diagram to outline how far society as a whole has come and where we, as individuals, fit within these steps. After the steps have been mapped, it will then be possible to pinpoint strategies that can help the new libertarian move from one stage to the next.

Konkin starts in "Phase Zero: Zero-Density Agorist Society". phase zero is the time when no agorists existed and libertarian thought was scattered and unorganized, which Konkin says has been "most of human history". Once libertarians became aware of the philosophy of agorism, counter-economic activity began and we moved into *"Phase 1: Low-Density Agorist Society"*. In this phase the first counter-economic libertarians appear. Konkin believed that this was a dangerous time for activists who would be tempted by *"Get-Liberty-quick"* schemes. Konkin also reminds agorists not to be tempted by political campaigns. *"All will fail if for no other reason than Liberty grows individual by individual. Mass conversion is impossible,"* he wrote.

Phase 1 is presented as a time when the few existing practicing counter-economists' main goal is recruitment and creation of *"'radical caucuses,' ginger groups, or as a 'Libertarian Left' faction in general"* (More on the "Libertarian Left" in chapter 5). Konkin also notes that the majority of society is acting *"with little understanding of any theory but who are induced by material gain to evade, avoid, or defy the State. Surely they are a hopeful potential?"*.

In order to achieve the free society, Konkin again emphasizes the need for education and *"consciousness-raising of counter-economists to libertarian understanding and mutual supportiveness"*. SEKIII also called for the creation of a movement of the libertarian left which may grow strong enough in influence and numbers in the latter stages of phase 1 to be able to *"block marginal actions by the state"*. The ability to block actions by the state has absolutely increased in recent years with the explosion of decentralized, peer to peer networks via the internet that allow for rapid sharing of information and calls to organize. There is a growing amount of internet videos showing communities banding together to oppose unjust arrests by agents of the State.

For example, the websites and apps *FreedomCells.org*, *NextDoor.com*, and *GetCell411.com* offer tools that can be used to strengthen our communities, grow the counter-economy, and push back against the state. Using *the Freedom Cell Network* one can locate other freedom minded individuals within their city, state, or country with the specific goal of organizing in the real world and bypassing the need for government. In 2016 we launched the site as an online platform for building mutual aid groups known as *Freedom Cells*, which we will explore in detail in the next chapter. *NextDoor* also allows the user to connect with the local community, both digitally and in the real world. The app has the added benefit of being focused on your specific neighborhood. This allows individuals to post important safety information, lost and found items, or counter-economic business opportunities, directly to those that live near them. Finally, *Cell411* describes itself as a *"real time, free emergency management platform"*. This means it allows you to create "cells" or groups to which you can send out direct alerts in the case of a flat tire, car accident, violence from a state agent, or some other emergency. The app also allows for truly agorist ridesharing where a third party does not dictate the price of the trip or the currency that must be used.

Each of these tools are a part of the technology of the counter-economy that have the potential to render government intervention and regulation completely useless. If we seize the moment we can grow the black and grey markets using these emerging peer to peer platforms. This is exactly what Konkin believed would help society progress from phase 1 to phase 2. As we move to *"Phase 2: Mid-Density, Small Condensation Agorist Society,"* the statists take notice of agorism. Is it in this phase that Konkin believes the counter-economy will grow and agorists will begin to represent "an ever-larger agorist sub-society embedded in the statist society". Although the majority of agorists are still living within the state's claimed territories, we begin to see a *"spectrum of the degree of agorism in most individuals"*. This includes benefactors of the State who are "highly statist" and "a few fully conscious of the agorist alternative", however, the majority of society is still engaged in the Statist economy.

From here, Konkin suggests that agorists may want to start condensing into districts, ghettos, islands, or space colonies. We are, in fact, beginning to see the creation of Agorist minded communities, sea-steaders, eco-villages, co-ops, and underground spaces which emphasize counter-economic activity and the creation of counter-institutions to the state. Konkin believed these agorist communities might be able to count on the sympathy of mainstream society to prevent an attack from the state. This is the moment where the question of community protection and defense comes into play. We have seen the creation of community protection alternatives to the police state monopoly (see *Threat Management Center* in *Detroit* and the *Autodefensas* in Mexico) but thus far nothing completely agorist has come into existence. It is the creation of these syndicates of community protection which will ultimately allow the agora to flourish. However, in order for this to happen *"the entire society has been contaminated by agorism to a degree"*, leading to the possible creation of an above or underground movement which Konkin called the *New Libertarian Alliance*. The NLA simply acts as the spokesperson for the agora and uses *"every chance to publicize the superiority of agorist living to statist inhabiting and perhaps argue for tolerance of those with 'different ways'"*.

This brings us to *"Phase 3: High-Density, Large Condensation, Agorist Society"*, which is described as the point when the state has moved into a terminal crisis period due, in part, to *"the sapping of the State's resources and corrosion of its authority by the growth of the Counter-Economy"*. As the agora grows in influence, the state's stranglehold is also dissipating as a result of unsustainable economic practices. Konkin again warns that the statists will attempt to win over new libertarians with "anti-principles" and calls for maintaining *"vigilance and purity of thought"*. Highly motivated new libertarians move into R&D to help create the first agorist protection and arbitration agencies that will compete with the state. At this point, government exists in pockets with the state mostly concentrated in one geographic territory. Those living under statism are very aware of the freedom being experienced by their agorist counterparts. The state has become weak enough that "large syndicates of market protection agencies" are able to contain the state and defend new libertarians who sign up for protection-insurance. This, Konkin believed, was "the final step before the achievement of a libertarian society." Society is divided between the larger agorist areas and the isolated statist centers.

The transition from phase 3 to phase 4 brings about *"the last unleashing of violence by the ruling class of the state"*. Konkin said that once the state's intellectuals recognize that their authority is no longer respected they will choose to attack. Defense against the state will be managed once the counter-economy has generated the syndicates of protection agencies large enough to defend against the remaining statists. The NLA should work to prevent the state from recognizing their weakness until the agorist movement has completely infected the statist society. Once the agorist communities have successfully resisted the state's attack the Agorist revolution will be complete. As we move from Phase 3 to 4, Konkin notes that the first three changes "are actually rather artificial divisions; no abrupt change occurs from first to second to third." However, he envisions the change from the third to fourth step to be "quite sudden".

Phase 4: Agorist Society with Statist Impurities

Once the State has gasped it's dying breath, the counter-economy becomes the freed market where exchanges are free of coercion. Konkin predicts that *"division of labor and self-respect of each worker-capitalist-entrepreneur will probably eliminate the traditional business organization – especially the corporate hierarchy, an imitation of the State and not the Market."* He imagines companies as associations of independent contractors, consultants and entrepreneurs. After the remnants of the state are apprehended and brought to justice, freedom becomes the basis of ordinary life and *"we tackle the other problems facing mankind".*

Whether the totality of Konkin's vision becomes realized, the world has, at the least, made some slight progress through the phases predicted in the NLM. All signs point to the counter-economy and consciously practicing agorist movement to be somewhere at the tail end of phase 1 and merging into phase 2. As mentioned above, the internet (and technology as a whole) has greatly increased the chances for success of the Konkian revolution. While mankind is being exposed to the value of a life free of coercion, they have not yet been properly exposed to the tools with which to create such a world. If the agorist movement and counter-economy continue to expand in equal rate to the violence and theft of the state, it will only be a matter of time before we see protection agencies with the capacity to defend the people. Konkin believed that once the people recognize the state is weakened and in decline they would naturally gravitate towards the counter-economy, leading his agorist vision to become reality.

To understand the potential for agorism to provide a solution to our current unsustainable, destructive system we must look to the real world. Political theories are fine on paper, but if the ideas don't reflect what we see in the physical world they serve as nothing more than mental masturbation. As Konkin wrote in the introduction to An Agorist Primer, *"Remember always that agorism integrates theory and practice. Theory without practice is game-playing; taken seriously, it leads to withdrawal from reality, mysticism, and insanity.....Agorists believe that any theory which does not describe reality is either useless or a deliberate attempt by intellectuals to defraud non-specialists."* So then, are there real world examples of counter-economics in practice? And if so, is there evidence that the practice leads to more freedom and prosperity?

To find an answer to these questions, let's look to the "informal sector" of Peru during the 1980's and 90's. The informal sector was made up of individuals who operated outside government laws and regulations. The activities of the informal sector are conducted outside the legal system without regard to government regulations. Collectively, the activities represent the informal economy. In his 1989 book, *The Other Path*, Hernando De Soto provides a detailed study of the emergence and operation of the Peruvian informal economy. De Soto argued that government regulations on housing, transportation, and trade should be removed to allow the dynamics of the informal economy to take over. Unfortunately, De Soto and *The Other Path* seem to equate capitalism with the free market, going as far as promoting "market-oriented reforms" which will allow the informal economy to become the new statist economy. Rather than promoting total liberation through the use of the informal economy and a truly freed market, De Soto and his Institute for Liberty and Democracy believe that a capitalist system of government will liberate the people. Despite these shortcomings, *The Other Path* is recommended for any student of counter-economic activity.

Another important point on Peru's informal economy is the fact that these black market entrepreneurs were investing in and creating informal businesses as a direct attempt to escape the regulations of the state, and the violence of the Maoist-terror group, "The Shining Path." When *The Other Path* was released it was designed to counteract the Marxist propaganda of The Shining Path, who had been teaching the peasant class the market was something to despise rather than a tool for liberation. The book would become a best-seller and help the growing informal economists recognize the power of unfettered trade and market action. Unfortunately, in the absence of a truly informed and organized agorist movement, the informal economy seems to have been absorbed by the Peruvian statist economy.

Still, during the rise of Peru's informal economy, the Institute for Liberty and Democracy reported that "extralegal entrepreneurs" and their extended families accounted for around 60 to 80% of the nation's population and operated 56% of all businesses. In the 2002 update to *The Other Path*, De Soto writes that the underground economies of Russia and Ukraine accounted for 50% of Gross Domestic Product, while 85% of all jobs in Latin America and the Caribbean were created in this informal or counter-economy. Obviously, the informal or counter-economy has become as important as Samuel Konkin predicted.

The Other Path not only highlights the importance of the counter-economy, but also illustrates how the state's restrictive and intrusive regulation of voluntary exchange directly lead to the growth of the underground markets. According to case studies conducted by the ILD, the average person attempting to launch a retail market in Peru during the 1980's would face 13 years of legal and administrative hurdles. In addition, it would take 26 months to get authorization to operate a new bus route, and almost a year, working 6 hours a day, to gain the necessary licenses to legally operate a sewing machine for commercial purposes.

"There is class warfare in Peru, to be sure. But the main line bisecting Peruvian society today is not a horizontal one dividing

entrepreneurs from workers. The principal dividing line is a vertical frontier, to the right of which are politicians, bureaucrats, and businessmen who profit and live off the government's favor and to the left of which are legal and extralegal producers who are excluded from favor," De Soto wrote in 2002.

Faced with ongoing violence and the Maoist rhetoric of The Shining Path on one side, and statist regulation and theft on the other, the people of Peru chose to travel to the countryside and create informal marketplaces for trading, ridesharing, and housing. This is what free thinking people will do when faced with the constant threat of theft and bureaucracy. Eventually, the people tire of having every aspect of their lives invaded by the state, so they will seek outside solutions. This may include reformist schemes like electoral politics and voting, or possibly violent revolt. Counter-economics and agorism offer a third path towards liberty. A path that is peaceful, consistent and reflects the realities we see unfolding in the world today.

There are also numerous documented examples of this counter-economic reality in China, North Korea, Cuba, and throughout Africa. Radical propaganda and Western media are smuggled into North Korea via USB drives while street vendors around the world operate without paying any mind to the state's permission slips. According to Kenya's National Bureau of Statistics, the informal sector created 713,000 new jobs in 2015, constituting a total of 84.8% of all new jobs created *"outside small scale agriculture sector and pastoralist activities"*. Further, in the book *Stealth of Nations: The Rise of the Global Informal Economy*, Robert Neuwirth documents the global reach of the counter-economy, or, as he calls it, *System D*. Neuwirth reaches the same conclusion that we have: people will organize outside of the state as a necessity, and, in many cases, with a preference for the untaxed, unregulated counter-economy.

It is clear that the workers of the world have a desire to exchange their goods and services without oppressive, elitist barriers to entry in the marketplace. The people desire to voluntarily associate and exchange without interference or intervention. This desire will always lead to the creation of counter-economic activity in the black and grey markets as long as the "mainstream" statist economy is subject to the whims of the current puppets in control. However, seeking to escape the state's regulation is not the only goal to our agorist and counter-economic strategy. The endgame is a stateless society where free people are not bound by the force and coercion of the parasitic state and corporate class.

Though it is rarely discussed in public schools or mainstream media, there are several examples of stateless societies and communities existing throughout history. For those interested in studying past stateless societies we recommend examining medieval Iceland, James Scott's *The Art of Not Being Governed: An Anarchist History of Upland Southeast Asia,* and Pierre Clastres' *Society Against the State.* We should also stress that those who believe a stateless society cannot exist because they do not see an abundance of examples, are only limiting themselves by setting preconceived barriers and assumptions regarding the potential of the human experience. If the hearts and minds of the world seize the opportunity and put agorist theory into action we will see the rise of the counter-economy. As we will explore in the next chapter, all it takes is a self-aware, organized agorist movement to seize the potential of the counter-economy and truly weaken the state.

Vertical and Horizontal Agorism

*"As more people reject the State's mystifications — nationalism, pseudo-Economics, false threats, and betrayed political promises — **the Counter- Economy grows both vertically and horizontally**. Horizontally, it involves more and more people who turn more and more of their activities toward the counter-economic; vertically, it means new structures (businesses and services) grow specifically to serve the Counter- Economy (safe communication links, arbitrators, insurance for specifically "illegal" activities, early forms of protection technology, and even guards and protectors). Eventually, the "underground" breaks into the overground where most people are agorists, few are statists, and the nearest State enforcement cannot effectively crush them."*

- SEK III, Applied Agorism, An Agorist Primer

We are going to take a look at two different types of counter-economic action which are applicable to a variety of individuals in a range of living situations. We refer to these strategies as vertical and horizontal agorism. We are working with two complementary definitions of horizontal and vertical which further explain the "how" of agorist philosophy. These definitions are taken from the above quote from Samuel Konkin III and from Swedish Austrian economist Per Bylund and his 2006 essay *"A Strategy for Forcing the State Back"*. Let's compare the definitions and see how they can provide a path for the eager agorist.

Konkin starts by describing the counter-economy as growing horizontally in the sense of an increasing amount of the mainstream population turning their activities towards the non-statist economy. Vertical growth, in the Konkian sense, involves the actual creation of counter-institutions to the statist counterparts. This means building alternatives not only to the economic power centers via alternative currencies, but alternatives to the deadstream corporate media, the corporatized food production systems, the compliant academic centers, and the growing non-profit industrial complex. *(Side note: the industry formerly known as the mainstream media is correctly referred to as the deadstream media because everything produced by this industry leads to*

misinformation, faulty decision making, and eventually, death. The
corporate media is a constant stream of lies and decay.)

Per Bylund describes his vision of vertical agorism as the
"introvert" strategy based on the work and ideas of radical libertarian Karl
Hess. Hess was an extremely eloquent speaker and speechwriter who grew
from conservative to libertarian anarchist to a more left-leaning
community organizer and activist. During the 1960's, he was heavily
involved in organizing on campus during the rise of the new left and anti-
war student movements. Hess worked with Murray Rothbard, Konkin,
Carl Ogelsby of the Students for a Democratic Society, and several others,
attempting alliances between the emerging new left and libertarian
movements. He was also one of the few people to have 100% of his wages
stolen by the IRS for challenging the income tax.

In the 1970's, Hess shifted the focus of his activism to experiment
in community building within the low income neighborhood of Adams-
Morgan in Washington D.C. In his books, *Community Technology* and
Neighborhood Power, Hess outlines how he worked with the local
neighborhood to build an empowered community focused on
sustainability, or what they termed "appropriate technology." Hess
describes a neighborhood with aquaponic gardening in basements, rooftop
gardens, and community services meant to replace the state option. He
was adamant that tools and technology directly contribute to freedom. By
being able to share tools with your community members, you are able to
share access to the means of production and encourage entrepreneurship.
It is this focus on community empowerment that Per Bylund refers to as
the vertical or introvert strategy. These actions can be considered agorist
in the sense that they are aimed at building self and community reliance
rather than dependence on external forces, but they are not explicitly
counter-economic because they do not involve black and grey markets.
Still, these vertical actions are extremely valuable and necessary.

Vertical agorism would include participating in and creating
community exchange networks, urban farming, backyard gardening,
farmers market, supporting alternatives to the police, and supporting peer
to peer decentralized technologies. While these vertical steps could
potentially involve the use of the state's currency (*and therefore not*

22

completely counter-economic) they are still significant for challenging the dependency on the state and corporate classes. Other vertical steps may not directly involve exchanging currency but still work against dependency. This could include moral support and promotion of technologies that disrupt the status quo and foster stronger relationships among community members.

One very pronounced example of vertical agorism is seen in the growing alternative media, which has been made possible by the internet. Less than one generation ago, the mainstream media, owned by mega-corporations and tightly regulated by government, controlled all of the information that filtered down to society. The distribution of information in society came from the top down, making it very easy to brainwash and propagandize the population. However, with the rise of the internet, activists and freedom seeking individuals discovered that they could use this new medium to create their own media, become journalists themselves, and fight back against the propaganda of the state. In just a few short years, the alternative media quickly upset the monopoly of the mainstream media, taking up large portions of their once exclusive market share. The surge of independent media provides an excellent example in our study of how alternative systems and institutions can be created to compete with existing state monopolies.

Our goal is to question and challenge the mechanisms of power that seek to influence and rule over our lives. This includes the state, as well as other institutions that attempt to exert control and influence. For example, by choosing to grow your own food or support local farmers you are taking a vertical step away from the biotechnology corporations that promote the heavy use of pesticides and a potentially hazardous technology. You are also not supporting the transportation of food products from thousands of miles away. Instead, you walk to your backyard or the local market for your produce. This greatly increases your independence while relinquishing support for an unsustainable industry. These vertical steps are also the easiest ways to begin living in line your principles. Once again, we can see the value of consistency of words and actions.

Per Bylund describes the horizontal, or extrovert strategy, as more directly related to the ideas of Konkin. The extrovert label is related to the bold choice to pursue action that the State considers to be illegal or immoral. By venturing into this territory you are joining the ranks of the bootlegger, the moonshiner, the cannabis dealer, the guerilla gardener, the unlicensed lawn mower, food vendor or barber, the weapons dealer, and the crypto-anarchists. When one combines the vertical and horizontal agorist strategy, an image comes into view that illustrates the steps that can be taken by a wide range of people in a variety of living situations and environments.

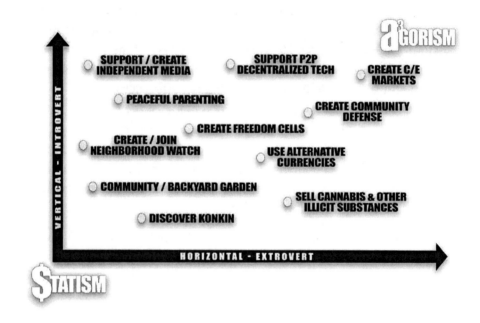

In the bottom left corner we have statism and in the top right corner we have agorism. We can plot vertical actions which help lift the individual up from dependency. Perhaps your situation is better suited to vertical actions such as growing your own food, using encrypted messaging, hosting community skill shares at your house, practicing peaceful parenting tactics, providing alternatives to state welfare by crowdfunding money for community projects and feeding the homeless, or simply cleaning up the neighborhood. Each of these steps move the individual (*and in the long-term, the community*) vertically towards consistency and independence. For those who are ready to become counter-economists and take on the risk of grey and black market activity, we plot their actions both vertically and horizontally. An agorist practicing horizontally and vertically would move up and away from statism and dependency to the top right position of agorism. This means for every garden built, alternative currency used, tax avoided, skill shared, business practiced without a license, and illegal substance sold, the individual can plot their progress moving from dependency to self-reliance and from statism to agorism.

When Konkin first espoused the concept of agorism, the consciously practicing counter-economy may have only involved a few radical libertarians, but since that time, the opportunities for black and grey market exchanges have grown immensely. As the state's weaknesses become apparent it will become safer for the masses to begin exiting the former economy and joining the counter-economy. This is the truly freed market, or agora, of which Konkin spoke.

Now that we have outlined the vertical and horizontal agorist strategy derived from the work of Karl Hess and Samuel Konkin, we must elaborate further on a concept that we hope will become widely adopted and adapted to many different communities. This is the aforementioned concept of Freedom Cells. Freedom Cells are peer to peer groups made up of 7 to 9 people (with 8 being ideal) organizing themselves in a decentralized manner with the collective goal of asserting the sovereignty of group members through peaceful resistance and the creation of alternative institutions. Freedom Cells could be seen as a very specific type of mutual aid group, where agorism and counter-economics play a key role. The name comes as a response to State propaganda around "Terror Cells". We are consciously choosing to reclaim the language and build cells that spread freedom. Also, FC's act like cells in a body that are performing important tasks individually while also serving the goal of the larger organism. In our vision, every FC is playing a vital role of spreading counter-economic activity and agorist philosophy while also forming a part of the larger network that will foster exchange of ideas and products between cells.

The number of 8 participants is drawn from the research of Bob Podolsky and his book *Flourish!: An Alternative to Government and Other Hierarchies*. Podolsky is the protege of researcher John David Garcia, who spent twenty years researching how to maximize the creativity of a group of people working together on a joint project. After performing hundreds of experiments, he came up with an optimized model based on groups of 8 that he called an Octet or Octologue. The idea being that a shortage of individuals would leave the group limited in capability, but with too many people the group is bogged down with disorganization and lack of focus. Podoslky recommends forming Octologues made up of 4 men and 4 women guided by specific ethical tenets.

Although Freedom Cells are also promoted as groups of 8 individuals collaborating together, they differ from Octologues in that they are heavily focused on decentralization. So while Bob Podolsky has outlined a detailed vision of how an Octologue should operate, we hope to provide examples of applications for FC's without telling other FC's how to operate. The needs of each community will naturally differ. Beyond a general agreement to respect each other's right to be free of coercion, we believe the FC's should not be monopolized by the vision of a single cell. We caution the reader to remember that our ideas are a guide, but not the final word on the literally limitless possibilities.

In the beginning, individuals can work together to accomplish goals such as every group member having 3 months' worth of storable food, encrypted communication, a bug out plan, and ensuring participants have access to firearms (or some form of self-defense) and know how to use them safely and proficiently. All the while, cell members make themselves readily available to render mutual aid to their cell, in whatever form that may come. Once you have established 7-9 people within a FC, each individual should be encouraged to then go on their own and start another FC, especially if the original members are not living in close proximity to one another. Living reasonably close to each other will allow for a quick response time in emergency situations. Once again, every member of the FC's should be encouraged to start additional cells.

Eventually, the original would be connected to 7 or 9 additional cells, through each individual member for a total of 70-90 people. Imagine the strength and influence these cells could exert once they are connected in the digital world via FreedomCells.org and in the physical world where possible. The creation of the Freedom Cell Network could also serve as social network for traveling agorists looking to do business in the counter-economy with other like-minds. Through building and supporting alternatives such as local food networks, health services, mutual defense groups, and peer to peer economies and communication networks, FC's will be better able to disconnect and decouple themselves from state institutions they deem unworthy of their support. Once groups become large enough in numbers, it becomes quite possible for participants to opt out in mass and secure their liberty.

This is the model we have been following in Houston with The Houston Free Thinkers activist community and The Free Thinker House community space. We began by building gardens and selling the crops via Next Door. We are also selling juice and kombucha tea using fruits harvested from trees of neighbors who understand our goals. We started with a small group of about 3 to 4 people meeting and discussing the goals and themes of our cell. The goal is to have skills and knowledge diffused throughout the group. This way, if one person leaves the group the knowledge is not taken from the cell. For example, knowing that every cell member can perform CPR, use encrypted communications, shoot a gun, or communicate the Agorist message may be important for your cell. Obviously, certain individuals will be more skilled or knowledgeable in some areas, but there are foundational skills and information that should be common among all cell members.

Our group has also used the structure to educate each other on specific topics of interest. Perhaps your FC meets and agrees to learn everything available on permaculture or a particular philosophical concept. You divide the topic up among your cell and return two weeks later to educate each other. Or maybe your cell joins the Cell411 app and responds to emergency alerts in your community. Several cells could join together to cop watch or actively resist and disarm violent police or other agents of the state. A Freedom Cell could connect with other cells for a covertly organized guerrilla gardening action. With the constant barrage of fake news coming from the establishment media, a FC could quickly research and debunk incoming propaganda. FC's can organize alternative exchange networks that encourage local artisans and entrepreneurs to come sell their unregulated crafts and accept alternative currencies. In a "Shit Hits the Fan" scenario, FC's could have pre-arranged bug out locations stocked with supplies. If several FC's were equally prepared, you now find yourself with a small community of empowered individuals as opposed to being forced to defend yourself alone.

These are the pockets of agorism that Konkin predicted would come as the counter-economy outcompeted the statist economy. While Konkin outlined his theory of getting from statism to agorism, he did not explore in detail the answer to how this would happen. We believe Freedom Cells are at least part of the equation. Konkin was correct in his prediction that the state would not hesitate to smash down any agorist who dared venture into the counter-economy too quickly or too boldly. This can plainly be seen in the punishment of Ross Ulbricht, the accused "criminal mastermind" of the Silk Road online marketplace.

Ulbricht helped people from all around the world do black market business without paying a single dime to the government of their respective homeland. Ulbricht and his apparent admin alter-ego Dread Pirate Roberts both expressed an affinity for the philosophy of agorism. When he was sentenced to three life terms in January 2015, the judge called his opposition to government and economic restriction "dangerous" and declared that she must make sure no one dare to "take up his flag". The state was quite literally terrified that the Silk Road allowed individuals to do business without their involvement. For all their alleged concern about the safety of drugs purchased on the Silk Road, the state truly opposed Ulbricht because it was a real-world practice in counter-economics designed to take power away from the state. In fact, drugs purchased on the Silk Road were far safer than those found on the street due to the reputation based rating and review system that was built into the site. Additionally, the online market removed the possibility of violence during the transaction, a danger that is all too real when buying drugs on the street.

Remember, we cannot defeat the Federal Reserve (or other central bank) by using their currency, this will only empower them. We must create and support alternatives to the state's monopolies whenever possible. It will take brave agorists venturing into uncharted territories, making mistakes, occasionally falling victim to the state's law, and learning how to better our approach. We need these pioneers to lay the groundwork so that others in the future will not have to face the same difficulties. As these trail blazers light the way we also expect to see a growth of free communities and freedom networks around the world.

We have a vision of thousands of interlocking autonomous communities comprised of empowered individuals with a variety of unique ideas and expressions of the human experience. Communities voluntarily trading and sharing skills without the violence inherent in our current paradigm. We believe this panarchistic, polycentric world can be achieved with an organized effort to spread Agorist philosophy and increase participation in the counter-economy via Freedom Cells and vertical and horizontal agorism.

We would like to offer these *"Ten tips For Building Freedom Cells"* as a starting point for launching your group. Please adapt these to the specific needs of your community.

1. Identify Potential Candidates - are they mentally, physically, spiritually sound for your goals?

2. Discuss Common Themes - what are the driving forces bringing the group together?

3. Identify Strengths and Weaknesses - take an honest look at the strengths and weaknesses of each individual, as well as the group as a whole.

4. Evaluate Desired Level of Freedom vs Security - Every individual may have a different desired level of freedom and as such, will have different aims and acceptability of risks.

5. Set Short Term and Long Term Goals - What can your cell accomplish in 3 months? A year?

6. Mindfulness Training - Incorporate practices like Non-Violent Communication Training and group meditation into your cell.

7. Accomplish Goals - Document each goal successfully met by the cell or individual members

8. Ongoing Group Education, Communication - continuously expand your cells knowledge, skills, and supplies.

9. Promote/Market Goals and Accomplishments - Use the power of social media (when safe) and marketing to let the world know how much more prosperous you are in the counter-economy.

10. Identify Strategies For Creating Income/Independence - Leverage the power and number of your cell to create counter-economic income that can't be taxed by the State.

Spontaneous Order In The Marketplace

When one examines many of the words used to describe our society, such as democracy, freedom, representative or capitalism, you find that these words are simply abstract euphemisms which are used to disguise the true authoritarian nature of our civilization. We are supposed to believe that "we the people" are represented by corrupt politicians, and that we are "free" despite constantly being exploited and ordered around by authoritarians. Much in the same way that we are told we are "free" in our personal lives, we are also told that we are "free" in our financial lives. Nothing could be further from the truth.

No matter what political system is employed by the ruling class the people are always faced with varying levels of subjugation. The word "democracy" is used to make our oppressive political system seem more benevolent and legitimate, while the term "capitalism" is used to give the impression that we operate under a "free market" economy. Neither are true.

Despite the many definitions of capitalism, it is generally associated with the rights to private property, private production of goods, and a "free market" economy lacking in state intervention. However, although the U.S. and many other western nations are thought of as capitalist, they typically fail to respect private property and promote heavy State regulation of economic exchanges.

At face value it may seem like capitalist economies represent a "free market", but when you take a look at property taxes, government subsidies for big corporations, and the mountain of red tape faced by entrepreneurs in these countries, it should become painfully obvious that a truly freed market has never existed under what most people identify as "capitalism". This is one of the many problems with associating the idea of a decentralized market of exchange with the system known as capitalism.

To those who would say the problem is a misunderstanding of capitalism we wish to reemphasize that capitalism, socialism, and communism have all been associated with statism and authoritarianism. This is an extremely important point, especially considering the fact that

31

so many anarchists are attached to one of these terms. Some are attached to the term socialism because they align with the stated goals of socialism, such as ending poverty. Meanwhile, others are attached to the term capitalism because they align with its stated goals of free enterprise and private property. However, with both of these systems, the stated goals are vastly different from the ends they achieve. For this reason and many others, these terms should be abandoned when discussing future concepts of non-statist economic systems.

The system that we have in place today, whether superficially appearing to be socialist or capitalist, could more accurately be called corporatism, mercantilism or cartelism. These words describe a system where the elite use their power in government to control the rest of society and prop up their corporate partners by eliminating competition through the political system. The monolithic corporations that now exist would have never been able to grow into what they are today without the help of government intervention and protection. Without government intervention, the infamous lobbyists in Washington would become obsolete because they would lose their power to influence and manipulate the marketplace through bribes or coercion. Government intervention and protection is the primary means by which the world's biggest corporations have devastated their competition and developed massive monopolies.

In a truly freed market there would be absolutely no need for a government, because any "service" that is provided by the government can actually be better handled by entrepreneurs. In today's system, we don't have independent businesses working on a level playing field. Instead we are left with a few massive corporations and cartels that use their power in government to maintain their monopolies and stomp out their competition. This is the very definition of fascism - the merger of state and corporate power - and it has become the dominant economic system in the world. Looking back through history, we can see that an elitist parasite class has always sought to use the state, religious organizations, and any other influential mechanism as a way to live off the wealth and surplus of the people.

Most of the "leaders" throughout the world propagandize the people into believing they live in a free and democratic society. This illusion pushes the masses to take their grievances to the polls like good citizens rather than taking their concerns into the streets or creating solutions that could actually make an impact. Currently one of the most totalitarian nations on Earth is called the "Democratic Republic of North Korea". Likewise, the government in America and the European Union are some of the most fascist regimes in history, yet claim to operate under systems of "capitalism" or "democratic socialism". It's a political word game that's designed to disguise the truth.

Almost every economic analysis in the world is dictated by the ideas of two long-dead aristocrats. On one end of the spectrum you have Karl Marx representing the labor theory of value and communism. Adam Smith can be found on the other end representing capitalism and "classical economics". Our whole way of doing business on this planet has changed very little since the time of these two men, and that could very well be the root of our problem.

Imagine how much we could accomplish if a few people in every city across the world wrote their own economic manifestos and gathered to respectfully discuss their ideas. The masses refuse to accept last generation iPods and video games, but without much thought, accept ways of living that are centuries old. It's time for us to work together to create strategies where everyone can meet their needs without violating the rights of others.

Capitalism and socialism are both terms that have been tainted by government and statism. They are terms that have been drug through the mud for hundreds of years and mean very different things to many different people. These differences in definition often make discussion of these terms impossible (especially on the internet!). We understand one could make the same argument regarding anarchism and it's unfortunate association with violence. While it is true that certain schools of anarchists who view violent revolution as a legitimate tactic, they are not the majority. Most freedom loving anarchists want to radically alter the systems of governance we have today, but do not advocate the force and violence we have seen displayed by those calling themselves socialists, capitalists, and communists.

Much of the money that is collected through taxation is used to line the pockets of politicians and establish bureaucracies that add to the size and power of government. A very small fraction actually ends up being spent on worthwhile public services. It should be obvious that if given the opportunity to allocate their own resources amongst themselves, communities would be able to provide services that are far superior to those that are forcefully imposed by central planners. Quite simply, our world does not need authority figures to dictate the course of human history.

The brutality and callousness of past regimes should serve as a constant reminder of how dangerous it is to give people authority over the lives of others. Rulers of the past have taken the credit for the hard work of the average people who have built civilizations on their command, leaving behind a historical myth that claims humanity owes its entire progression to kings, priests, politicians, and other authoritarians. In reality, we have the ingenuity of our ancestors to thank, not the tyrants who rode on their backs. The history books may glorify warlords, monarchs and aristocrats as being the founders of our modern way of life, but this is only the result of the victorious warlords writing the history books.

Many world changing inventions, enlightening philosophies, and leaps in human development have been brought forth by those who spent their lives under the boots of authority, not those wearing the boots. Historically, authority figures have actually done their best to hinder this process and prevent the general population from empowering themselves with technology and philosophy.

The power structures of the past were well aware that the peasants had the potential to rise above oppression peacefully through the advancement of philosophy and development of advanced technology. This was very pronounced during the times of the Middle Ages where people could lose their lives on counts of witchcraft if they were caught developing unknown technology or discussing any philosophy that may have undermined the existing establishment. Frederick Douglass stated that when he was a slave in the American south he was not allowed to learn how to read a calendar, or even know how old he was. The power structures of the world today are no different. They prevent research into alternative energy and alternative medical treatments, and stifle technological advancement with stiff regulations and intellectual property laws.

There have been periods in history of significantly less government intervention in the economy, but these situations could hardly be referred to as "free market". As long as we are subject to central banks, government mandated currency, taxation, bailouts, and regulations, we are dealing with a very tightly controlled market, not a free one. Through the government mandated schools and regulated media we are presented a story where economic sanctions and controls are necessary to keep people safe from the evil corporations who have monopolized the economy. This is a pretty clever trick because most people fail to take a few steps back to see that these corporations have been created and protected by government. In fact, many corporations are exempt to the regulations and taxes that are hoisted upon the smaller businesses who are trying to compete.

These are the policies that have created the completely unjust and unsustainable economic environment that has forced so many people into poverty and despair. Companies like Monsanto and Goldman Sachs would not survive a day in a truly freed market that lacked the political mechanisms they currently use to stomp out competition. They would be forced to depend on the support of the community and the integrity of their product. Fortunately, in the face of more honest and efficient entrepreneurs, corporations like Monsanto would be exposed and fall flat on their faces. The very concept of a "corporation" is a government created entity which acts as a legal shield to keep CEO's from being held accountable for the messes they create. These legal loopholes have allowed the monopolization of certain industries, creating mega corporations that no legitimate small business can possibly contend with. The state education system and corporate media keep the public in the dark by failing to acknowledge that our current economic model is a result of government intervention.

In a world where people were actually allowed to trade freely without 3rd party intervention, everyone would be an entrepreneur. Sure, workers would still be needed, but our guess is that in a free society most labor jobs would be filled with people trying to earn extra money - working a summer job, getting some startup money for their own business, a teen working their first job, and things of that nature. It seems that the "wage-slave" model of working a dead end job for your entire life is due to a lack of choices currently in the marketplace. There is something to be said for picking up a skill and sticking with it throughout the years, but in a truly decentralized and free economy there would be more of a potential to start your own business which could then employ others.

A group of entrepreneurs would also have more freedom to band together and form a commune, co-op, or mutualist enterprise. We believe that a freed market would favor non-hierarchical worker owned businesses. People are always free to enter whichever types of arrangements they prefer, but we predict that most people would likely prefer not working under authoritarian bosses. This preference for non-authoritarian work would lead some to gravitate towards horizontally owned businesses or entrepreneurship. Even in today's industries, businesses where workers have a share in the spoils of the company tend to be far more successful and offer better customer service because the employees have more of an incentive to do a good job rather than just punching a clock.

The point is that without the state intervention and the propping up of corporations that do nothing but feed the consumerist frenzy, we would see a decrease in the need for pointless labor. We reject the notion that being a worker simply for the sake of work is virtuous. When it came to the working class, Konkin also argued that the state stifled innovation and entrepreneurship which kept the working class busy doing meaningless busy work. He called workers and peasants *"an embarrassing relic from a previous age at best and look forward to the day that they will die out from lack of market demand"*. Indeed, with technological growth pushing farther towards automation, the menial jobs done by most workers could be done by artificial intelligence, paving the way for existing workers to become entrepreneurs.

In the world we are describing, the quality of life and creativity on the planet would explode and create a dynamic civilization with the

36

potential for peace and abundance. Different currencies could be tested all throughout the world while new ways of doing business and structuring society would develop in different areas until the optimum solution for health and wellbeing was discovered. These ideas would be voluntarily adopted by the masses because of the value added to their lives. This vision is possible.

By now it *should* be common sense that initiating violence greatly diminishes the quality of any situation or relationship. Violence may seem to be a strong word to describe government policy, but legitimized threats of violence backed by the guns and prisons of the State are still acts of violence. If you disobey the government for too long or with too much fanfare the end result is ultimately your death. By breaking the laws of the government you will likely find yourself in their court system. If you choose not to participate they can send out men with guns to your house to take you away and put you in a cage. At that point if you refuse to go they will use force on you, and if you attempt to defend yourself you will be killed.

The state wants the public to believe that only a guilty party resists an arrest. But what if that arrest was really an unjust kidnapping? Who is to say that the court issuing the charges is legitimate? Were the courts and laws in Soviet Russia or Nazi Germany legitimate? Were the people who disobeyed them guilty of a crime? Putting on a uniform and working for the king, the sheriff, or the president does not grant you the right to kick down the doors of nonviolent people and attempt to kidnap them.

This systemic violence disrupts the process of spontaneous order by stifling human will power and creativity. Spontaneous order is a way of describing the complex building process that takes place all throughout nature, as well as in interactions between human beings. When applied to human interaction, this building process is set into motion by people trying to solve problems and improve their quality of life.

Human beings have an incredible ability to find solutions for any problems that may stand in our way. Just as a rushing river will forge a new path around a boulder that has fallen in its midst, groups of voluntarily cooperating people (Freedom Cells) will naturally find a way around any roadblock when they have a desire to do so.

The phrase *"where there is a will, there is a way"* is extremely relevant in this context and describes the process of spontaneous order and self-organization in a most concise way. It can be difficult for some to see this unfolding in nature because of how our day to day lives are compartmentalized and separated from our actual needs. Due to this compartmentalization, many of us have come to believe that there will be no food if the grocery store closes down, there will be no electricity without a government power grid, and that there will be no safety without the king's guards patrolling the community. However, all of these needs can be handled more proficiently by the open hearts and strong minds in our community. Without a state to hold us back we will witness spontaneous order and self-organization within the agora.

Agorism is not Anarcho-Capitalism

The goal of this essay is three-fold. First, we will identify the key concepts which outline the philosophy of agorism and the strategy of counter-economics, as outlined by Konkin in *The New Libertarian Manifesto* and *An Agorist Primer*. Second, we will illustrate how radicals of all stripes can utilize the strategy of counter-economics, as described by Konkin, without necessarily endorsing his philosophy of agorism and its specific tenets. Finally, we will describe what sets agorism apart from anarcho-capitalism and other schools of thought. We will show that although the counter-economic strategy can be utilized by nearly any individual, agorism itself is not simply a strain or subset of anarcho-capitalism, as some believe, but rather, it a unique political philosophy of its own which can be used by anarchists of any economic background.

Before we dive in, allow us to briefly explain the inspiration for the title of this essay and the essay itself. As we will demonstrate, the agorist message and counter-economic strategy can be of use to any individual who finds themselves in pursuit of a more free, just, and ethical world. However, the reason the title focuses on anarcho-capitalism is because we have noticed a trend in "right-libertarian"/AnCap social media circles where individuals claim to support the ideas of Konkin and his agorism, yet also express a distaste for left-libertarianism. Our goal is to help readers with this viewpoint understand the essential role Konkin and his "new libertarianism," or agorism, played in developing the American left-libertarian movement.

Agorism As Consistent Libertarianism

Let's start by getting an understanding of Konkin's vision. Konkin called for the creation of a revolutionary movement lead by workers and entrepreneurs voluntarily cooperating in economic exchanges that take place outside of the state's grasp. He called this movement The New Libertarian Alliance. Konkin based his revolutionary ideas on a foundation of libertarianism in the vein of Rothbard and the American individualist anarchists before him. In *The New Libertarian Manifesto* Konkin writes:

"Where the State divides and conquers its opposition, Libertarianism unites and liberates. Where the State beclouds, Libertarianism clarifies; where the State conceals, Libertarianism uncovers; where the State pardons, Libertarianism accuses.

Libertarianism elaborates an entire philosophy from one simple premise: initiatory violence or its threat (coercion) is wrong (immoral, evil, bad, supremely impractical, etc) and is forbidden; nothing else is.

Libertarianism, as developed to this point, discovered the problem and defined the solution: the State vs the Market. The Market is the sum of all voluntary human action. If one acts non-coercively, one is part of the Market. Thus did Economics become part of Libertarianism."(1)

From this, Konkin developed his views on property:

"Libertarianism investigated the nature of man to explain his rights deriving from non-coercion. It immediately followed that man (woman, child, Martian, etc.) had an absolute right to this life and other property – and no other.

All theft is violence initiation, either the use of force to take property away involuntarily or to prevent receipt of goods or return of payment for those goods which were freely transferred by agreement." (1)

Konkin became involved in the burgeoning libertarian movement in the late sixties. At this point the lovers of liberty were beginning to recognize the potential for a national movement of anti-statist, pro-market radicals. In the midst of this opportunity, Konkin saw libertarian activists being lured into "get liberty quick" schemes in the name of pragmatism, such as electoral politics. In a counter-attack to the enemies of liberty, Konkin outlined a new philosophy that he believed was simply the result of applying libertarian principles to their most consistent and logical ends.

"The basic principle which leads a libertarian from statism to his free society is the same which the founders of libertarianism used to discover

the theory itself. That principle is consistency. Thus, the consistent application of the theory of libertarianism to every action the individual libertarian takes creates the libertarian society.

Many thinkers have expressed the need for consistency between means and ends and not all were libertarians. Ironically, many statists have claimed inconsistency between laudable ends and contemptible means; yet when their true ends of greater power and oppression were understood, their means are found to be quite consistent. It is part of the statist mystique to confuse the necessity of ends-means consistency; it is thus the most crucial activity of the libertarian theorist to expose inconsistencies. Many theorists have done so admirably; but we have attempted and most failed to describe the consistent means and ends combination of libertarianism.

New Libertarianism (agorism) cannot be discredited without Liberty or Reality (or both) being discredited, only an incorrect formulation." (1)

For Konkin, a truly libertarian society would be agorist – *"libertarian in theory and free-market in practice"*. This society would include a respect for justly acquired property, voluntary cooperation between entrepreneurs and producers, and replacing all of the state's "services" with private competition among individuals and collectives.

"Libertarian analysis shows us that the State is responsible for any damage to innocents it alleges the 'selfish tax-evader' has incurred; and the 'services' the State 'provides' us are illusory. But even so, there must be more than lonely resistance cleverly concealed or 'dropping out?' If a political party or revolutionary army is inappropriate and self-defeating for libertarian goals, what collective action works? The answer is agorism." (3)

The goal of agorism is to replace all non-consensual, coercive relationships with voluntary relationships based on mutual benefit via entrepreneurship in the black and grey markets. This shuffling of *"large collections of humanity from statist society to the agora"* was *"true revolutionary activity"*. According to Konkin, agorists should not launch "attacks" on the state. *"We are strictly defensive,"* Konkin wrote in *An Agorist Primer*.

Further, Konkin described an agorist as *"one who lives counter-economically without guilt for his or her heroic, day-to-day actions, with the old libertarian morality of never violating another's person or property"*. The philosophy stresses the importance of taking action. *"An agorist is one who lives agorism. Accept no counterfeits. There are agorists "trying to live up to it." There are, of course, liars who will claim to be anything. As Yoda said so succinctly, 'Do. Or do not. There is no try.' That's Agorism."* (4)

Counter-Economics As Defined by Konkin

If Agorism is Konkin's premiere philosophical contribution, his recognition of counter-economics as the path towards agorism is equally important. The term counter-economics can be attributed to the time and period in which Konkin developed his ideas. *"Counter-Culture was a popular phrase, the only lasting victory of the "hippies." Counter-Economics implied that the "revolution wasn't finished" and that the Economic System needed to undergo the same up-ending as the Culture had,"* Konkin wrote.

As defined above, the black and grey markets are part of the counter-economy, which Konkin defined as *"All (non-coercive) human action committed in defiance of the State"*. In line with the principles of non-aggression, Konkin labels initiatory violence in the form of theft or murder as the "red market", the one type of activity that is shunned in his counter-economy. Konkin explains that as the State's repressive and oppressive activities increase, the people will begin seeking economic alternatives to State regulation and interference. This provides an opportunity for forward-thinking agorists to launch and support counter-economic businesses and activity. Konkin believed that once the counter-economy had progressed to the point where entrepreneurs were providing the public with protection and security services that could rival or defend against the state, the agorist revolution would be complete.

"Slowly but steadily we will move to the free society turning more counter-economists onto libertarianism and more libertarians onto counter-economics, finally integrating theory and practice. The counter-economy will grow and spread to the next step we saw in our trip backward, with an ever-larger agorist sub-society embedded in the statist society. Some agorists may even condense into discernible districts and ghettos and predominate in islands or space colonies. At this point, the question of protection and defense will become important."(3)

"Eventually, of course, after a period of increasingly rapid change of this kind, the "underground" will break into and displace the "overground"; the state will wither away into irrelevance, its taxpayers, soldiers, and law-enforcement people having deserted it for the marketplace; and we'll be left with a free, agorist society." (4)

Counter-Economics As A Tool For All Radicals

Konkin envisioned a world of decentralized, peer to peer communities consciously and voluntarily doing business in the counter-economy as a means towards ending the state and liberating the people. The range of (and opportunity for) counter-economic activity has only increased with the expansion of the internet and decentralized technology like crypto-currencies. Konkin discussed various forms of counter-economic activity including, using cash to avoid detection, barter, investing in precious metals, undocumented employment, use of illicit and illegal drugs and medicines, prostitution, bootlegging, gambling, weapons dealing, or simply providing a service while accepting payment in non-statist currencies.

The possibilities are essentially endless and should be welcomed by all radicals who are seeking alternatives to statism and the status-quo. Any individual or collective who recognizes the economic monopoly that is maintained by continued use of the Federal Reserve note should be supportive of counter-economic measures and investing in creating alternatives. Whether your idea of economic freedom is collective ownership or individualist in nature, agorism offers an opportunity for communes, mutual banks, time stores, and marketplaces based in the counter-economy. This will allow all non-statist counter-economic ventures to cooperate and compete in the pursuit of a more free society. As we note in our first book, there is there an opportunity for the creation of an agorist-mutualist alliance and some agorist theorists are even calling for an agorist-syndicalist alliance. Quite simply, if you want to abolish the state and the privileged class who benefit from its existence, create alternatives to the current paradigm and outgrow the archaic institutions of yesterday.

We should note that Konkin was critical of communism. In *"Counter-Economics: Our Means"* he writes, *"the anti-market commune defies the only enforceable law – the law of nature. The basic organizational structure of society (above the family) is not the commune (or tribe or extended tribe or State) but the agora. No matter how many wish communism to work and devote themselves to it, it will fail. They can hold back agorism indefinitely by great effort, but when they let go, the 'flow' or 'Invisible Hand' or 'tides of history' or 'profit incentive' or 'doing what comes naturally' or 'spontaneity' will carry society inexorably closer to the pure agora."* (3)

Understanding Konkin's Vision of Agorism

It is important to distinguish counter-economic activity from full on agorist activity. While one may be a drug dealer, prostitute, arms dealer, barber without a license, or other grey/black market entrepreneur, it does not follow that one is also a consciously practicing counter-economist or agorist. Generally, economic activity in the black and grey markets is always counter-economic because it is untaxed and removes the state from the situation. But, without the awareness of agorist philosophy and conscious effort to remove economic power away from the state, one is simply breaking the state's law. While flouting the state's laws against victimless crimes is a commendable act, it does not make one an agorist. In short, you can support and participate in counter-economic ventures without wholeheartedly embracing Konkin's ideas, but you would not be an agorist.

So what differentiates agorism from anarcho-capitalism and other forms of market-anarchism?

As noted earlier, Konkin was a vital part of the establishment of the left-libertarian movement of the 1960's, 70's, and 80's. The Movement of the Libertarian Left was born of Konkin's experiences working with Murray Rothbard and Karl Hess on Left and Right, a journal dedicated to bringing together the anti-statist "right" and new left of the late 60's. These experiences greatly influenced Konkin's thinking and development of agorism. When asked why he chose to identify as a "libertarian left" or left-libertarian, Konkin said he was "to the left" of Rothbard, so it became natural to refer to the his movement as left-libertarian. He also noted his interest in continuing "Rothbard's 1960-69 alliance with the anti-nuke, then anti-war New Left".

"Among important figures in the development of the modern libertarian movement, Konkin stands out in his insistence that libertarianism rightly conceived belongs on the radical left wing of the political spectrum," writes David S. D'Amato for Libertarianism.org *"His Movement of the Libertarian Left, founded as a coalition of leftist free marketers, resisted the association of libertarianism with conservatism. Further positioning it on the left, agorism embraces the notion of class war and entails a distinctly libertarian analysis of class struggle and stratification."*

When asked about the main differences between left-libertarian/agorism and anarcho-capitalism, Konkin said, *"In theory, those calling themselves anarcho-capitalists do not differ drastically from agorists; both claim to want anarchy (statelessness, and we pretty much agree on the definition of the State as a monopoly of legitimized coercion, borrowed from Rand and reinforced by Rothbard). But the moment we apply the ideology to the real world (as the Marxoids say, "Actually Existing Capitalism") we diverge on several points immediately."*

In Konkin's words, *"the "Anarcho-capitalists" tend to conflate the*

Innovator (Entrepreneur) and Capitalist, much as the Marxoids and cruder collectivists do. Agorists are strict Rothbardians, and, I would argue in this case, even more Rothbardian than Rothbard, who still had some of the older confusion in his thinking." Konkin also said the AnCaps of his time had a tendency to *"believe in involvement with existing political parties"* and using the *"U.S. Defense complex to fight communism"*, terrorism, or any other misguided cause. While it may be said that AnCaps who support the Defense Department are a minority in 2017, the point does illustrate that since the beginning of the agorist movement there has been an effort to segregate from the AnCap element. With a growing segment of today's AnCap movement being in favor of using state violence to enforce immigration and "protect" cultural conservatism, it makes perfect sense that Konkin wanted to separate himself and his movement from such positions, despite the overlap between the two philosophies.

Konkin believed *"a lot more than statism would need to be eliminated from individual consciousness"* for a truly free society to exist. Based on this statement (and his writings elsewhere) it seems clear that Konkin espoused a "thick" libertarianism that fights for collective liberation through individual means and does not end its analysis at statism or property rights. Indeed, Konkin specifically wrote about the oppression waged against women and the gay community, something often ignored or explicitly avoided by many AnCaps. Another difference between Konkian libertarianism and that of "right-libertarians", is the issue of class. Although the right typically avoid class-based analyses, Konkin helped develop what has become known as "The Agorist Class Theory". The Agorist Class Theory refutes Marx's communist class theory and recognizes the differences between non-statist entrepreneurs and statist-capitalists.

Konkin elaborated on these ideas in an interview and in discussions on the left-libertarian Yahoo group. Again he stressed the importance of separating the *"non-innovators, and pro-statist Capitalists"* from the *"non-statist Capitalists (in the sense of holders of capital, not necessarily ideologically aware)"*, calling them *"neutral drone-like non-*

innovators". Additionally, Konkin made favorable comments towards workers movements. In the left-libertarian Yahoo Group, Konkin said he approved of the Industrial Workers of the World's (IWW) attempt to recruit libertarians. Konkin said he wanted *"to remind old MLL members and inform newbies that, free-market and pro-entrepreneur as we are, MLL supports genuine anarcho-syndicalist unions which consistently refuse to collaborate with the State. (In North America, that's the IWW and nothing else I know of.)"* He noted that the IWW split with the U.S. Socialist Party for the same reasons his MLL split with the U.S. Libertarian Party – *"a rejection of parliamentarianism for direct action".*

Konkin also disagreed with conflating the terms "free enterprise" and "capitalism" with the "free market". *"Capitalism means the ideology (ism) of capital or capitalists,"* he wrote. *"Before Marx came along, the pure free-marketeer Thomas Hodgskin had already used the term capitalism as a pejorative; capitalists were trying to use coercion — the State — to restrict the market. Capitalism, then, does not describe a free market but a form of statism, like communism. Free enterprise can only exist in a free market."*

Konkin referred to his movement as "revolutionary" and "radical", terms that are generally used to describe left-leaning movements, and rejected by "right-libertarians" and conservatives. The use of terminology from the new left was not a mistake. Konkin was consciously making an effort to distinguish his brand of "revolutionary market-anarchism" from the growing anarcho-capitalism movement, which came to be associated with political action and cultural conservatism. In his time, Konkin saw many Ancaps as "sell-outs" who avoided revolutionary activity due to its social and legal risks while opting for ineffectual, vanilla lifestyles, more in line with the conformity of mainstream, statist society.

In conclusion, Samuel E. Konkin III successfully created an extension of libertarian philosophy by utilizing tactics that are consistent from theory to application (Counter-Economics) while providing a path towards a more free society. He made efforts to acknowledge the differences between his movement and others, but at the same time recognizing that the counter-economic attack can be waged by a wide spectrum of anti-Statists. If we can successfully create a panarchist alliance of counter-economists, we may yet construct a truly freed market that allows free experimentation and trade between different schools of thought. In this space we will see the conscious agorist movement flourish.

Part 2: Our Vision of a Stateless Society

Providing Public Services Peacefully

The time has come to start thinking unconventionally when considering alternatives to the current methods of funding community projects. As it stands right now our civilization is forced to fund projects involuntarily through coercive taxation. The force and violence involved with the collection of taxes is only scratching the surface of the negative consequences that this practice has on our society. Let's take a moment to hash out the implications of coercive taxation.

Since the government is allowed to extract money from the people by force, this guarantees they will have funds for any project they want, even if those projects are unpopular with taxpayers. This is because the public has no choice but to pay taxes, therefore they have no say in how their money is used. Thus, the tax-paying public (*and not the agorist!*) end up paying for their own oppression and unjust wars around the world. Sure, there are some social welfare programs that assist people, but the cost of these projects are a tiny fraction of the money that is actually received via taxation. Most of the money that is stolen through taxation is used for bureaucratic budgets, collection enforcement, and the gluttony of federal and state governments. So while a portion of the revenue is being used for beneficial projects, a majority of the money is still being wasted or used for nefarious purposes. Imagine a thief giving you five dollars while also taking a hundred dollars from your back pocket.

One of the most common complaints about the government is that it does not truly serve the public. The reason for this is simple: the government gets paid regardless of whether or not the people are satisfied. This means they have no incentive to actually listen to the public they depend on for funding. Likewise, the disharmony between the state and citizen inevitably leads to mismanagement, violence and corruption. On the other hand, if community projects were funded through voluntary means people would only pay for the services they wanted. This would likely lead to a lack of funding and the eventual collapse of authoritarian governments as they were faced with either extracting funding from the public using physical force or adjusting their own behavior. Under these circumstances wars would be prevented, small businesses would have an easier time competing in the marketplace, and trillions of dollars in wasted overhead would either be back with its rightful owners or used in beneficial social projects and programs. If someone wanted to invade territories halfway around the world or put together an oppressive bureaucracy like the Department of Homeland Security, they would lose funding because most people would not willingly support their authoritarian adventures. This is the whole concept behind voluntarily funding community projects: good service will render payment from the public, while poor service will lead to a lack of a customer base and thus a lack of funding.

There is an unbelievable amount of fear directed at this concept because for most of history our civilizations have been propelled by violence, instead of a balance of compassion and logic. Immediately upon hearing about these ideas of doing away with coercive taxation, many people who are new to the idea will immediately scoff, *"if taxes were not collected under threat of force then no one would pay them! There will be chaos and the poor will die in the streets!"* It's time to recognize that forced taxation isn't working for the average person and ideas like *"the consent of the governed"* and *"the social contract"* are complete fallacies. We must acknowledge that there is a growing discontent among Americans. The two corporate political parties are losing support and people are losing faith in the system itself. Do we really think that the public would choose to sign a contract agreeing to have one third of their earnings stolen to pay for the government's actions? If not, then it surely cannot be said that the system of involuntary taxation is any type of consensual relationship. And if the relationship is not consensual and voluntary, then it is not legitimate.

If tax revenue was put into projects of value to the people they would be more likely to voluntarily contribute money. Although our culture projects a pretty bleak view of human nature, our world is filled with a diverse spectrum of people who are kind and care a great deal about their neighbors. Recent studies have even shown that compassion might be hard-wired into the human genome. Einstein believed that, *"If people are good only because they fear punishment, and hope for reward, then we are a sorry lot indeed"*. So while it is true that people are naturally driven by incentives, most people also exercise empathy for their fellow human beings and are driven to help others when possible. In fact, helping others and the emotional reward it provides is often the incentive needed to drive people to help others. In fact, in 2010, people gave over 290.89 billion dollars to charity. This is after the public has already been mugged for one third of their income by the government, and in the middle of the worst economic conditions since the great depression. Imagine how much they would have given had they been able to keep all of their income and had the reassurance of knowing their money was actually being spent correctly. Not to mention, imagine if all the money the public gives to wasted political campaigns was redirected to projects that the community actually wanted.

There is currently a lack of confidence in the ability of charities to support our needs - and with good reason. Many non-profits have succumbed to the corruption of our culture of dominance and become part of the non-profit industrial complex, the unfortunate outcome of well-intentioned activists who become entrenched in bureaucracy. However, according to 2008 data from *Charity Navigator*, an average of 80-85% of the money that is donated to charities actually ends up in the hands of the needy. That same report goes on to quote several sources who found that the government takes over 70% of all tax revenue collected and uses it for their own public funds, salaries, military projects, and wasteful bureaucracies. They also found that less than 30% of public tax revenue is actually spent on the public. It was even suggested by 1984 U.S. Grace commission that nearly every dollar of income tax collected in America funds political corruption and pays the debt to the Federal Reserve. So even in today's world of "sub-par charities" those charities outcompete the State when it comes to improving the condition and lives of those in need. These charities accomplish all of this on a voluntary basis, without threats, violence, or tax collectors.

There is no need to force compassion and anyone who claims that charity must be forced does not have your best interest at heart. The myth that the public benefits from taxation is just an elaborate advertising scheme that attempts to justify its existence. Even mobster Al Capone ran run soup kitchens in Chicago so the people would overlook his crimes and see him as a charitable man. The government takes the same approach by spending some of their pocket change on welfare programs and community projects, but all of this is only done out of an obligation to maintain the appearance of effective management of tax revenue. In a free society where public services and community projects were funded voluntarily there could be various community groups that gather to discuss the issues important to the community at large. These meetings could be open to everyone and facilitated by alternating community members. These brainstorming sessions would allow the community to present suggestions for the allocation of resources. All suggestions would need to comply with the sovereignty of the individual. As mentioned earlier, FreedomCells.org and NextDoor.com could help organize these meetings.

There could be essential life-saving programs that would always be receiving donations, and available to everyone in the community - whether they donate or not. Since these areas were so vital to life they would likely receive the funding needed due to the high value of the service. For example, water treatment plants, fire fighters, or community gardens would have no problem with funding because they are in high demand.

When it comes to community defense, the public generally blindly puts their faith in the police and military. As with all other mechanisms of the state, these organizations are monopolies rife with corruption and inefficiency. Despite these obvious truths, the propagandized masses continue to credit these institutions for holding our society together. The popular misconception is that without forcing people to pay for these monopolies there would be chaos and danger. However, other models for community defense are entirely possible without the need for state-sanctioned theft. Under the current paradigm, if you are upset about police corruption you cannot simply stop giving them your tax dollars and search for another security provider. Instead of waiting for the state to fix the problems, there are private citizens taking matters into their own hands by organizing to provide security for their community. A great example of a currently existing alternative to the police can be found in Detroit. To counter the notorious corruption and ridiculously long police response times, Dale Brown formed the "Threat Management Center" in areas of Detroit where police don't answer 911 calls. Brown's organization fights crime, offers free protection for victims of domestic violence, and is also able to service poor areas of Detroit for free by charging a premium to work security in the city's richest neighborhoods.

Two other important areas of debate related to providing services in a world without involuntary taxation are the roads and the courts. When it comes to courts, the vast majority of civil disputes, especially in the world of business, are actually handled by non-government arbitration services. There is no reason why criminal cases cannot be handled in the same fashion. Anarchists who do not wish to use force to collect money for "the public good" are often asked *"who will build the roads?"*. Apparently, there are those who believe in the absence of the State humanity will suddenly become incapable of laying down a dirt path or connecting roads into an interstate freeway. These people discuss the creation of government roads as if the construction was simply due to the kindness of government and not made possible by the theft of taxation. However, what the government really does is collect money from private citizens under the threat of violence, then use that money to employ those very same citizens to build infrastructure. The reality is that the people could build infrastructure themselves for less money if they coordinated with neighbors and other communities. In other words, if they just cut out the middleman. This exact scenario played out in 2009 on Hawaii's Kauai Island when private citizens performed a $4 million road repair job for free in 8 days.

Beyond the basic necessities, a myriad of secondary programs and services from transportation, internet, and space exploration could also be funded through voluntary donations from the community. Remember, as a result of the lack of overhead and enforcement costs which inflate all bureaucratic budgets this would likely be cheap in comparison to the prices that we see today on public projects.

Some may be concerned that it would be hard to achieve community goals on a voluntary basis, but this would actually improve the efficiency and value of public services. Oftentimes government funded jobs don't even see completion! It is unbelievably common for Western governments to start popular programs during election years to gain public support, only to later pull the plug so the funds can be used for wars or bailouts. This kind of manipulative behavior takes place all the time. However, when there is a project that has enough support, it will usually receive sufficient donations from individuals, businesses and charity organizations to keep the program operating. This can clearly be seen in the explosion of online crowdfunding websites and campaigns. We also saw this in the US in 2011, when the government pulled the plug on funding for the SETI space program in the midst of a half dozen wars and major austerity measures. This was a program that the public felt so strongly about that over 2,000 donations were received in a single week, easily surpassing their goal of $200,000.

If we think about this same problem presenting itself in the potential free society that we are discussing, we can easily assume that it can be solved in a similar fashion. Except this time around, there will be far less overhead and people will have more to give to the cause, thus ensuring a greater success rate than we see today under the rule of the State. If people stopped contributing to a certain program, that program would put out word to its supporters to raise the extra funds needed to carry on the project. This is the wonderful thing about how our species self-organizes and uses their intelligence and resources to solve problems when they appear.

When a need arises in a community, people naturally and spontaneously come together to take care of what needs to be done. They don't need a bureaucrat with a gun in their face forcing them to do it. For our species to have a future we must start thinking about more peaceful ways of doing business. We must stop justifying the use of violence in all circumstances - even "soft-core" violence like government legislation, taxation and indoctrination.

Stewardship of the Earth

Regardless of your thoughts on anarchist or statist theory, every single human being on this planet needs clean water and the fruits of the Earth to survive. The Earth is our home and our source of life and it is not something that is promised or guaranteed. This simple fact has been overlooked by our species as unsustainable practices continue to destroy our planet for the short term gains of an elite few.

The negative relationship that our species has with the Mother Earth is without a doubt driven by the authoritarian control structures and economic systems that dominate the world. If there was an award for the planet's biggest polluters, the governments and militaries of the world would undoubtedly take the prize, along with their corporate friends. In addition to making a mess of the world on their own, global governments suppress clean and renewable energy technology, which in turn forces the rest of us to use unhealthy products that damage our bodies and environment.

There are several competing philosophical views when it comes to the environment and the concept of ownership. We cannot deny that our species' time here on this planet is finite, while the Earth will be here for many, many future generations. With that being the case, it hardly makes sense to consider ourselves the owners of the land, the water, or other resources which predate and will outlast our existence. We take a view of the ownership of the Earth that could be more correctly termed stewardship. Essentially, each of us are caretakers of the life on this planet, whether we choose to accept the role or not. This does not mean that all claims to property should be abandoned, but it does imply a certain amount of personal responsibility in relation to the living standards of future generations. We must acknowledge that for much of recent history humanity has been a poor caretaker of the planet. Still, we reject the notion that government bureaucracy is the answer to destruction of the environment.

Ironically enough, it is the governments and international governing bodies in charge of protecting the environment who are largely responsible for the dismal condition of our habitat. It is often the state and scientific establishment that push the propaganda that the average citizen is the source of all of our environmental woes. In June 2015, a group of scientists from Stanford University, Princeton University, the University of California, Berkeley, and others warned that the Earth is experiencing a sixth mass extinction era. They called for fast action to save endangered species and habitats. The scientists claimed that species' are disappearing at up to about 100 times faster than the normal rate between mass extinctions, known as the background rate. Their study was published in the journal Science Advances.

The researchers told Stanford that their estimates were conservative and that the situation may be much worse than previously believed. *"We emphasize that our calculations very likely underestimate the severity of the extinction crisis, because our aim was to place a realistic lower bound on humanity's impact on biodiversity,"* they wrote. Paul Ehrlich, the Bing Professor of Population Studies in Biology, a senior fellow at the Stanford Woods Institute for the Environment, and co-author of the study said, *"[The study] shows without any significant doubt that we are now entering the sixth great mass extinction event."*

Of course, it is absolutely important for free hearts and minds to strive to live an existence that is in balance and harmony with the planet and all the life we share this space with, and it is true that this is not currently happening. Environmental damage is taking place, but the study ignores the impact government institutions have on the environment and it places the blame solely on the average consumer. While it is true the average consumer does play a role in environmental pollution, their impact is miniscule in comparison to that of governments and major corporations. Also, one of the reasons the average consumer uses toxic products in the first place is because more sustainable alternatives are forced off the market.

Also, Professor Ehrlich's involvement might set off a few alarms for those familiar with the topic of eugenics. Eugenics is the belief that humans can be "improved" or controlled through genetic or social engineering. In 1981, Ehrlich wrote the book, *Extinction: The Causes and Consequences of the Disappearance of Species.* Before that, Ehrlich co-wrote *Ecoscience,* which sheds some light on his ideas. Published in 1977 with John Holdren, former Science Czar for the Obama Administration, *Ecoscience* promotes a number of radical ideas for dealing with the world's population. Some of these ideas include forced abortions enforced by a global police force, which requires the loss of individual sovereignty. Quite simply, these people want the public to believe that humanity is a disease, something to be managed, controlled, or eliminated.

The same people responsible for most of this environmental degradation also create nature based foundations and other phony environmental organizations. These organizations are used to stash money and often advance eugenics depopulation programs. The ruling class understands that human beings naturally have an interest in preserving the environment and that most people will typically not question or criticize actions taken in the name of environmental protection. The latest scheme of the ruling class is exploiting environmentalism and fears of "global warming" to establish a carbon credit taxing system. The rationale of this theory is that human beings are creating environmental destruction via their use of carbon, so the suggested solution is to tax the average people and control their energy use. If climate change is actually a result of manmade carbon output then surely taxation wouldn't be a realistic solution, yet according to the establishment this is the ONLY possible solution.

Yet, the average citizens aren't responsible for the majority of the world's environmental destruction, nor are they responsible for the majority of the world's carbon output. In fact, the 50 largest transport sea vessels produce more carbon than all the cars in the world. These are military vessels, oil tankers and other transport vehicles for corporations and governments.

Howard Zinn's incredible research in *"A People's History of the United States Of America"* reveals that, *"In 1992 more than a 100 countries participated in the earth summit environmental conference in Brazil. Statistics showed that the armed forces of the world were responsible for two thirds of the gases that deplete the ozone layer. But when it was suggested that the earth summit consider the effects of the military on environmental degradation the United States delegation objected and the suggestion was defeated."* The general public is not to

58

blame for the environmental crisis that stands before us. We have inherited it from the careless governments and corporations who suppress alternative energy sources and are responsible for the vast majority of the world's pollution.

The perpetrators of these crimes place the blame everywhere but themselves, and use their political power so they can actually benefit from all the destruction they are causing. Al Gore was one of the most prominent spokesman for the carbon based global warming theory. He is also one of the primary advocates for a worldwide carbon tax and is closely involved with businesses that stand to reap large profits as a result of possible carbon tax schemes. He says his motivations are to reduce the energy uses of the general public, but according to the Tennessee Center for Policy Research, he has a mansion in the Belle Meade area of Tennessee which consumes more electricity every month than the average American household uses in an entire year.

When this information went public, he defended himself by saying that he pays a "carbon offset", but what he didn't say is that he paid it through a company that he owned called Generation Investment Management. In other words, he paid the money to himself! Al Gore became a proponent of a carbon tax via his good friend and founder of the embattled Enron Corporation, Ken Lay. This makes perfect sense considering the fact that Enron was an energy company which had very close ties in Washington, and was notorious for concocting deceitful schemes to fleece the public out of their hard earned money.

To make matters worse, most of the evidence paints a picture quite different from the "official" stance on global warming. The earth's temperature and climate has been changing and fluctuating since the beginning of time on account of various factors, namely solar activity. Drastic changes in weather have been recorded throughout history and some would argue these changes are a natural process. To claim that a natural process that has been happening forever is evidence of a recent threat defies logic. Since the "Climategate" scandal broke in November of 2009, the carbon based global warming theory has lost support and is now under extreme public scrutiny. Although politicians and mainstream media sources claim that there is some sort of a scientific consensus on this topic, there still exists a reasonable amount of skepticism within the scientific community itself.

While all of this discussion and controversy is taking place over this very specific theory, there is a list of other environmental issues that are being ignored. Our energy resources are being poorly mismanaged by the organizations that control them. These governments and corporations are destroying the planet and placing the blame on us so they can justify making us foot the bill. The abundant use and lack of long-term studies on genetic engineering and pesticides has created new species of weeds and pests that pose an unprecedented threat to our ecosystem. Toxic radiation and pollution has become commonplace in our everyday environment, mostly due to corporate carelessness and military exercises. There are very serious environmental issues that we need to correct, but it's not limited to one chemical compound and we aren't going to solve anything by taxing the average consumer.

Without a doubt, the Earth is suffering. The planet is ravaged with environmental disasters, loss of important ecosystems and species, and a population that seems increasingly ignorant to the impact it is having on the rock they call home. Every free mind should work to live in harmony with this planet and reduce the impact of our existence on this beautiful, unique place we call Earth. That is without question. What we should question, however, are the motives for governments and other parasitic classes who promote the idea that humanity is the problem that needs to be corrected.

Another recent environmental issue which divided activists (particularly the American Libertarian movement) was the 2016 fight against the Dakota Access Pipeline near Cannonball, North Dakota. The DAPL, alternatively known as the Bakken Pipeline, is owned by the Dallas, Texas based corporation Energy Transfer Partners. The pipeline is slated to stretch 1,172 miles upon completion and transport crude oil from the Bakken fields of North Dakota to Patoka, Illinois. The project is set to cross the Missouri River not far from the Standing Rock Sioux Reservation in North Dakota. The Standing Rock Sioux claim that the U.S. Army Corps of Engineers violated the National Historic Preservation Act by not properly consulting them before approving the project. The

Sioux filed suit against the Army Corp and in April 2016 launched the Sacred Stone Spirit Camp as a site of a resistance to the pipeline. Protesters, allies, and journalists came from all around the world in support of the Spirit Camp, as well as additional camps that were launched in support including the Red Warrior Camp, Rosebud camp, and Oceti Sakowin. Beginning in August 2016 the number of tribes and indigenous communities standing in solidarity with the Standing Rock Sioux grew to over 500. The coming together of such a large number of tribes, many of whom have been enemies in the past, was a historic event in itself.

Beyond the lack of consultation with the natives, the water protectors (as the Sioux and allies prefer to be called) were fighting against the property claims of the U.S. government. Technically (according to the U.S. government) the water protectors in the Oceti Sakowin camp north of the Cannonball River were on private property owned by the U.S. In October 2016, the protectors launched an additional camp closer to the construction of the pipeline. The Sioux called this the "Treaty" or "Frontline Camp" named for the 1851 Laramie Treaty under which the Sioux still maintained ownership of the land. The Sioux stated that they were implementing their own form of eminent domain and retaking the area because the U.S. government has failed to abide by its own treaties.

In order to prevent the completion of the pipeline, which the Sioux and water protectors see as not only a violation of treaties, but an attack on the water and planet, the camps were willing to risk arrest by using direct action to physically stop the construction of the pipeline. Some critics of the water protectors argue that they are in the wrong for going on private property and "forcing" the cops to use violence in defense of said property. We completely disagree with this misguided view. Anarcho-capitalists, libertarians, conservatives, and other propertarians who take this position are completely ignoring the history of broken treaties between the U.S. and indigenous communities of the landmass currently known as North America. This is particularly disturbing to see coming from followers of Austrian economist Murray Rothbard. Drawing on John Locke's homesteading proviso, Rothbard argued that individuals who mix their labor with unused property can become the legitimate owners. *"The homesteading principle means that the way that unowned property gets into private ownership is by the principle that this property justly belongs to the person who finds, occupies, and transforms it by his labor,"* Rothbard wrote in *"Confiscation and the Homestead Principle",* (The Libertarian Forum, June 15, 1969). *"This is clear in the case of the pioneer and virgin land. But what of the case of stolen property?"*

Rothbard goes on to say that when dealing with stolen property one must make an effort to find the legitimate owner. This means the original person who homesteaded the land or the person who legitimately acquired the property from that original owner. If unable to locate the original owner the person who was last in possession of the property without the need for statist privilege becomes the proper owner. While we have criticisms of other stances taken by Rothbard (particularly his stances on agorism, cultural issues, and his later adoption of paleoconservatism) we agree with him on this issue. This means that Energy Transfer Partners, the U.S. Army Corp of Engineers, and private citizens who sold their land for the pipeline cannot be considered the legitimate owners of the land in question. Especially, not when this land has historically been used by the Sioux nation and was only acquired by any agency of the U.S. government through violent wars and broken treaties. Rothbard also responds to the critics who believe that the water protectors should respect the private property rights of the oil company and attempt to fight the battle in court.

"What of the myriad of corporations which are integral parts of the military-industrial complex, which not only get over half or sometimes virtually all their revenue from the government but also participate in mass murder? What are their credentials to "private" property? Surely less than zero. As eager lobbyists for these contracts and subsidies, as co-founders of the garrison state, they deserve confiscation and reversion of their property to the genuine private sector as rapidly as possible. To say that their "private" property must be respected is to say that the property stolen by the horsethief and the murdered must be "respected.""

Frankly, these corporations do not have rights and should not be granted the same property protections as people. Without subsidies and State granted privilege, these corporations would not to be able to maintain their monopoly on energy. The corporate Oilgarchy and their state partners also work together to suppress alternative energy technologies that have the potential to outcompete the oil barons. Another point of contention in the DAPL debate has been the fact that the movement views itself as defenders of the sacred Mother Earth and natural resources. The fight between the water protectors and the Oilgarchy is best seen as a cultural divide. The indigenous people of this planet tend to think in terms of the principle of the 7th generation. This means that one considers the effects of their actions on not only the next generation, but the 7 coming generations. This perspective differs greatly from the opposing view that could be termed the "Modern" or "Western" worldview which tends to focus exclusively on the here and now. It is this type of thinking that perpetuates the use of oil and other invasive, unsustainable products.

The water protectors, specifically the indigenous communities, are fulfilling their spiritual commitment to defend the land and the water. Many of them do not care about debates over whether the direct action was a violation of property norms. These are individuals who are often willing to die in defense of the planet. We believe this is an honorable position that could be supported while still being consistent about not initiating force or even violating property rights. For example, one could argue that a homesteader who causes irreversible harm to their property is initiating force against future generations of property owners and the planet itself. Additionally, damage done to one piece of property will undoubtedly lead to contamination of adjacent properties due to the interconnected nature of the environment. What this means is that polluters themselves are actually committing the first act of aggression, and would thus open themselves up to consequences from their neighbors.

We believe this position is sound based on property claims as well as an argument for defending the undefendable. In book 1 of this series, we mention the need for humanity to rethink our relationships with non-human animals and the planet. We discussed the implications of consciousness and rights applied to animals and the environment. Although some will argue that animals are incapable of rational thought and therefore incapable of being considered anything other than property, we have come to the conclusion that animals should be given equal status to children, the elderly, adults with diminished mental capacity, or similar vulnerable groups incapable of self-defense and reason. With each of the groups it is generally accepted that a guardian or agent of the vulnerable individual would be justified in defending them against the initiation of force. This same logic can be applied to animals and potentially the Earth, in reasonable circumstances.

For example, if you witness your neighbor abusing their dog for no good reason you may feel called upon to ask them to cease and desist. If that fails you could gather your freedom cell and issue a warning. If that also fails to end the violence you may consider physically removing the dog from the abusive owner. If the owner views his dog as property, he may consider you to be aggressing upon his legitimate claim to ownership and choose to respond violently. At this point we have two individuals who believe they are in the right. This situation could be arbitrated between competing insurance agencies, but would likely lead to one agency recognizing the rights of animals and the other agency denying such protections. Until there is a global shift in the perspective of our relationship with animals we are likely to see a continued debate over whether they are property. Still, we were drawn to anarchism because we desire a world without systematic, publicly accepted violence. Viewing animals as property to be used for entertainment is the type of thinking that leads to orcas trapped in captivity at SeaWorld, and miserable animals held prisoner in zoos. *Should we not hold ourselves to a higher standard and live a compassionate life in balance with the animals and the environment?*

We are not advocating a fascist vegan takeover where every individual is forced to abandon meat eating. In fact, one of the authors of this book is vegan, and the other is not. We don't have any intention of sending one another to the gulags or re-education camps. However, we do advocate a more conscious relationship with the animal nations and the Earth. We also call on those concerned with dangers to the environment and animals to boycott factory farming industries, including most mainstream restaurants, and non-organic, non-local produce which involve the heavy use of dangerous pesticides. Mass factory farms are damaging to the surrounding environments and also perpetuate the disturbing slavery and abuse of animals bred to feed the human population. Not to mention that animal agriculture is responsible for a large portion of greenhouse gas emissions. If you want to fight deforestation and carbon emissions stop supporting animal agriculture.

Statism is also responsible for propping up the corporations involved in industrial farming and animal agriculture. Without statism and with an increase in the counter-economy and agorist localization, factory farms (and the abuse to the environment and animals caused by them) would be greatly reduced. If we grow the urban farming and backyard gardening movements we could decrease the need for such unsustainable and violent industries. This won't be a perfect vegan world where no one eats meat, but it would greatly reduce the acceptable level of violence used against animals and the Earth.

Our final point relates to the question of who is best suited to tend to the local environment. The common refrain from the authorities is that the people are ill equipped to handle management of local resources and protection of the environment. We are told that without a government the environment would become sold off to the highest bidder and polluted. However, recent research seems to contradict these claims. A July 2014 report from the World Resources Institute and the Rights and Resources Initiative found that communities take better care of forests than governments. The report, *Securing Rights, Combating Climate Change*, reviewed over 130 earlier studies in 14 countries to see the effect of community management of resources. According to the report, areas of the Brazilian Amazon under control of the indigenous communities saw a deforestation rate of .6 % while government held areas were at 7%. In Guatemala, the rate of forest loss in government-protected areas was 20 times that in areas under community control. The World Resources Institute report confirms a 2012 analysis by the Institute of Ecology which found that on average, government-protected tropical forests were cut down about four times as fast as community-managed ones. Finally, the work of Elinor Ostrom perfectly illustrates the benefits of community environmentalism versus state environmentalism. Ostrom, winner of the Nobel prize for economics in 2009, found that problems with resource management occur when outside forces, including governments and well-meaning conservationists, intervene.

It is clear that humanity needs to reevaluate our relationship with the planet and all of its inhabitants. Rather than looking to governments or elites to save the day, we should be focused on how we can take action that will defend the livelihood of those living today and future unborn generations. This action may sometimes involve directly challenging the mechanisms of power that attempt to damage and control the planet in ways that affect our very existence. We should strive to remain consistent with our goal of not initiating violence while at the same time standing strong as warriors in defense of the Earth.

The Authoritarian Right and Left

There are several different examples of political spectrums in use today. Most people in the U.S. measure the political parties and philosophies across a horizontal line, from liberal to conservative. Others see the political spectrum as a square with totalitarianism in the top corner and freedom in the opposing corner. We tend to disagree with most political spectrums because they misunderstand the eternal struggle of freedom versus tyranny and mistakenly believe that either the right or left side is closer to freedom, or that one is better than the other. This tyranny manifests itself as non-voluntary communism, statism, fascism, imperialism, and any other form of authoritarianism. The opposite of all these power schemes is anarchism.

In the realm of politics, economics, and religion there exists many "false dichotomies" in which there seems to be a narrow field of two options to choose from. In reality, there is actually a larger set of possibilities beyond the pre-approved guidelines. In other words, you are asked to choose between black and white, leaving you to think that the only colors in existence are black, white and maybe gray, when in reality there is a whole palette of different shades and tints that are completely left out of the discussion. The statement, *"If you're not with us, then you're against us"* is a classic false dichotomy, because it only presents two options, both of which amount to violence, while completely neglecting the possibility of remaining neutral. Likewise, the traditional left/right paradigm is also a false dichotomy which forces people to choose between two seemingly different, but equally authoritarian sides.

Anarchists should not make the mistake of believing that they are a part of "the left" or "the right". These terms are skewed beyond repair and have different meanings in different nations and at different points in history. Alliances with right and left have failed every time because ultimately the followers of the corporate political parties are still playing into the mainstream paradigm. This leaves them open to manipulation and adopting what Konkin called anti-principles. The mainstream left and right will always sell out the principled, but misguided anarchists who seek alliances with one side over the other. We should absolutely reach out to both the right and the left and attempt to bring our message to them as much as possible, but we must be careful not to sacrifice our principles. We should work to bring them towards our principled stance. Rather than believing the answer lies in one end of the political spectrum, freedom minded individuals should work to ally with like-minds from all sides. The danger is in believing that one end of the spectrum holds the one path to liberty and that the other side is the problem. This is the same false dichotomy that we sought to escape when we first abandoned the left/right paradigm and mainstream politics.

After waking up to the reality that the Democratic and Republican parties are controlled, many free thinkers have taken to a life of activism in hopes of changing the world. However, many of these people who broke through the mainstream left/right paradigm are now falling for another false paradigm leading to the same cycle of frustration and division that is seen in the mainstream political circus. The legitimate frustration felt by those seeking solutions has caused some on both the left and the right to become even more extreme in their dogmas and in their support of government. These individuals fail to remain consistent and instead fall prey to the deception of Statism once more.

An interesting aspect of the political spectrum in America is the fact that it is constantly changing and shifting. In America, Democrats and Republicans regularly trade positions and switch stances on important issues. For example, for a period of time after World War 2, prior to the red scare and the Cold War, the Republicans were known to take strong anti-war positions. The red scare and Vietnam War pushed conservatives towards a more pro-war position while the Democrats reacted in opposition, and subsequently became known as the anti-war party during the era of the new left. In reality, neither corporate party is truly anti-war. They simply adopt anti-war rhetoric to gain the support of people who wanted peace. In terms of economic policy, "liberals" were traditionally advocates of free markets, while in today's political climate most identifying with that label advocate strong government control of the economy. What this tells us is that both ends of the spectrum do not stand on principles, but are constantly manipulated by media hype, the whims of politicians, and calls for "pragmatism" in the face of both real and imagined political or cultural enemies.

In America, this has resulted in what has come to be known as the "Alt-Right" on one side and the "Social Justice Warriors" (SJW) or *regressive left* on the other. Many of those who now identify as Alt-Right came out of the 2008 Tea Party movement and the subsequent growth of the American Libertarian movement fueled by Presidential candidate Ron Paul. The former Congressmen from Texas was a student of Murray Rothbard and has actually been very outspoken against the Alt-Right. After the Libertarian movement failed to capture the presidency and end statism, many activists found themselves disillusioned with not only the political system, but with libertarian principles. Whether or not these people ever truly understood the message is debatable, but in the end this crowd went on to support Trump and has come to be associated with wanting to violently impose their vision of "freedom". The Alt-Right has become obsessive with combatting their enemies: leftists, commies, "cucks", SJWs and anyone else who does not support their heavy handed vision of society. In their obsession with their enemies they have lost sight of the goal of freedom.

On the other side of the spectrum are the social justice warriors, the hyper-vigilant group who focus on identity politics and seek to use the force of government to censor free speech in the name of political correctness. This group is constantly looking to shame any real or imagined instance of racism or bigotry. This often has the unintended consequence of emboldening bigoted people and taking attention away from legitimate instances of hate and bigotry. This group's roots are in the progressive movement that believed the election of Barack Obama in 2008 was their moment. After eight years of expanding the wars, the surveillance and police state, targeting whistleblowers, and corporatism, the progressives lost faith in Obama. Many of this same crowd had their bubbles burst once more in the summer of 2016 when "Independent" Democratic Presidential candidate Bernie Sanders handed his revolution over to Democratic nominee Hillary Clinton. Now they spend their time focusing on micro-aggressions, "call out culture", and the bigotry of their perceived enemies on the right. Just like the Alt-Right, they have become obsessed with their "enemy" and have lost sight of developing solutions to the two-party system.

The left and right fear one another so much that they end up embracing the rhetoric of dictators in order to vanquish their political enemies and save their version of civilization. It is common for those on the left to venerate historical dictators like Stalin or Mao, and now increasingly common for the alt-right to embrace murderers like Chile's former dictator Augusto Pinochet. In fact, many in the alt-right, and even some confused anarcho-capitalists have recently been promoting the idea of throwing political opponents or "counter-revolutionaries" out of helicopters into the ocean, an inhumane practice that was notoriously employed during Pinochet's reign of terror. They justify this outright call for violence by citing insidious libertarian infiltrator Hans-Hermann Hoppe's "physical removal" proposal. Hoppe is a conservative monarchist who masquerades as an anarchist and espouses authoritarian views that are in total opposition to true libertarian values. In his book *"Democracy, The God That Failed"* Hoppe outlines his vision of a "free" society:

"One may say innumerable things and promote almost any idea under the sun, but naturally no one is permitted to advocate ideas contrary to the very covenant of preserving and protecting private property, such as democracy and communism. There can be no tolerance toward democrats and communists in a libertarian social order. They will have to be physically separated and removed from society."

Hoppe goes on to express his distaste for "alternative", non-traditional lifestyles:

"Likewise, in a covenant founded for the purpose of protecting family and kin, there can be no tolerance toward those habitually promoting lifestyles incompatible with this goal. They–the advocates of alternative, non-family and kin-centred lifestyles such as, for instance, individual hedonism, parasitism, nature-environment worship, homosexuality, or communism–will have to be physically removed from society, too, if one is to maintain a libertarian order."

What Hoppe is describing is obviously a dictatorship, yet his supporters will insist that these types of aggressive tactics towards political enemies are necessary in order to save "western civilization." Hoppe's supporters have also said that he is being misinterpreted, but it seems fairly clear he imagines physically removing people from his ideal society, not just his own property. It is important to point out that Hoppe has a massive body of work, most of which does not promote this type of hateful strategy of exclusion, but these passages soil the rest of his work, and leave a dark cloud over libertarianism as a whole, so we cannot with a clear conscience reference or promote his work in a positive light.

One common refrain from the alt-right is that they are here to save western civilization, or white culture, or European values, while disparaging "Eastern civilization". This outlook tends to mask bigoted views and completely ignores the violence of the West and the accomplishments of the East. In reality, both eastern and western cultures are responsible for great achievements and systematic violence.

Essentially, the philosophy of the alt right is that state violence or private violence is justifiable and necessary against political opponents who have ideologies that are deemed to be threatening or dangerous. According to their logic, the ideologies of their political enemies, whether it be communism, environmentalism or whatever, are viewed as acts of aggression in themselves, and thus they believe that they would be defending themselves by using violence against their enemies. While it may be true that certain ideologies can be precursors for acts of aggression, simply holding an idea is not an act of aggression, and does not warrant a forceful response.

This illogical sophism is not exclusive to the right either, leftists are regularly justifying violence against political enemies who have not aggressed against them, but have merely espoused views which they find threatening. This was seen clearly during protests surrounding the 2017 inauguration when white supremacist Richard Spencer was punched by a black-bloc protester while he was being interviewed on the street. The attack was largely celebrated by left leaning activists who felt that Spencer's ideology was an act of violence which justified a forceful response. This is, of course, the same argument that the authoritarian right uses to justify violence against their political enemies. Spencer's ideas may be absolutely disgusting, but if we allow violence to be used against his ideas, then that means anyone can arbitrarily decide that an idea is a threat to their existence, and then use philosophy to justify violence on any person they choose.

On the other hand, when Richard Spencer crosses the line from simply talking about having a white separatist community to wanting to physically remove or exterminate people of color, that takes a step closer to what we call aggression. No physical act of violence has been taken, but a threat has been issued. When someone has made it clear they want to use violence against you, do you allow them to grow in influence to the point that they might actually be able to get away with violence? Or do you preemptively attack them to stop their growth? And at what point do you decide to move? Should it be once they have become backed by the force of law? If so, we would argue that criminals are already in power and thus violence could be justified against them. We do not think such an action would achieve the goal of a free and ethical society so we choose not to initiate force. But some might propose that statism is such a threat that they should use violence against those who vote. On other end of the spectrum someone might say that Anarchists are a threat to "law and order" so violence is justified against them. You see where we are going with this. This is a slippery slope that leads to barbarism and a reversal of our progress as a species. Remember, good ideas do not require force. We can convert hearts and minds with reason and logic, as well as leading by example.

Just after the attack on Spencer at the 2017 inauguration, he attempted to infiltrate the International Students for Liberty Convention, and notable libertarians in attendance showed us exactly how someone like him should be handled. When Spencer attempted to set up his own speech outside the event, he was confronted by a large group of conference attendees, including Jeffrey Tucker, Will Coley, and others, who challenged Spencer's ideas, and told him that his fascist views were not welcome at that property. Spencer called for a police escort and quickly left the building without incident.

Both the Alt-Right and the SJWs are guilty of collectivizing their enemy and refusing to judge each individual according to their own behavior. This division can even be seen within the alternative and independent media. Journalist outlets once responsible for hard-hitting investigative news are now simply perpetuating the same false dichotomy while pretending to be anti-establishment, as they too have fallen victim to the trap of division. Sadly, the alternative media has become no different than the divisive corporate media, with extremists on both ends having endless arguments and rarely discussing solutions.

In the end, the mainstream political left is manipulated by their compassion while the right is manipulated through their desire for independence. Compassion and a pursuit of independence are both admirable qualities, but both can be used against us. The right perceives compassion as negative because they can see how the left is manipulated, but at the same time, they do not see how they are being manipulated through their desire for independence. Likewise, the left perceives independence as negative because they see how it is used to manipulate their political enemies, but they cannot see how their compassion is used against them.

Both sides play into the hands of the establishment by advocating violence and division, and in this sense these groups work towards the same ends despite any apparent superficial differences. It is possible for rational people to be both compassionate and independent without being manipulated by government or being divided amongst one another.

The hate and division seen in politics should make one thing extremely clear: It is not a good idea to force large populations of people in a specific geographical location to live under the same rules, adhere to the same culture, fund the same projects and so on. People are unique individuals with a broad spectrum of beliefs and values. For optimum peace and prosperity each of these unique individuals should be able to live according to those beliefs and values, so long as they do not impede on their neighbor's freedom to do the same.

Panarchist Experiments:

Can Propertarians & Non-Propertarians Co-Exist?

Centuries ago most people would have thought it was impossible for two people who belong to two different religions to be neighbors, yet it happens every day in modern society. In this same way, it is possible to envision a future world where neighbors have different concepts of economics, culture, and politics, and are still able to live in peace. If we aim to create a stateless society, we must understand the potential hurdles and pitfalls that we may experience along the way. As we have studied revolutionary movements of the past, several areas of concern have consistently appeared in our research. We hope to remedy these complex situations by providing a balanced perspective into how people of varying beliefs can co-exist.

As we have made clear in the previous chapters, we believe society is capable of spontaneously organizing without the need for central authority or government. However, one of the biggest roadblocks to achieving this goal comes from within the "radical" movements themselves. Namely, the conflict between those who believe private ownership of property is itself an act of violence or theft, and those who believe private property norms are the key to a free society. These different camps have vastly different ideas about economics and culture, which puts them at odds and make it very difficult to form alliances, despite a common enemy in the state. However, these differences are not irreconcilable, and it could be possible for these groups to live side by side if they both adopted an attitude of mutual respect.

Regarding the title of this chapter, *Can Propertarians and Non-Propertarians Co-Exist?,* we do not intend to argue in favor of complete private ownership or total communal ownership of resources. Our goal is to illustrate that co-existence based on mutual respect and a recognition of individual sovereignty is possible. Many anarchists of the past have sought to determine who is right or wrong in property claims, and who has the moral high ground. These contributions are valuable, but they have already been discussed at great length in various social circles and publications. Our goal here is not to determine blame or moral high ground, but to predict how free humans would handle disputes in the most civil way possible, since peaceful resolution is in everyone's best interest. This is not to say that morality is relative or a matter of opinion, morality is a very real and objective thing that centers around the use of force. However, we recognize that not everyone is going to share the same views on topics like this, so it is important to determine how this disagreement could be rectified peacefully.

We believe in panarchism, a true marketplace of ideas where all forms of governance and anarcho-hyphens can compete and cooperate to their liking. During the transitionary period between the state's total collapse and the establishment of new free communities and collectives, there is great potential for a power vacuum as opposing groups attempt to gain a foothold in the post-state world. However, we predict that this potentially violent period will be short as people realize that peace and cohabitation is in their own self-interest.

If the battle with the state was particularly grave it is highly unlikely that the people will want to continue to wage bloody conflicts among themselves. This is not to say that conflicts will be non-existent, but we believe mutual respect will make for more manageable conflict resolution. The anarchists involved in the Spanish revolution of 1936 were ultimately crushed by competing factions of communists and statists. This lesson should not be forgotten. Still, we should strive for common ground because the other option is endless conflict. The world is a beautifully diverse place and will always be so. If we cannot compassionately debate differences of opinion we are doomed to repeat our violent past. As noted in the last chapter, authoritarians of all stripes buy into the illusion that they can force the world to conform to their particular worldview and values, but this is an impossible task, even if one end in the conflict does have the moral high ground.

So then, how do we go about achieving this state of mutual respect and healthy conflict resolution? We believe the answer lies in the work of Josiah Warren, America's first individualist anarchist, abolitionist, and founder of anarchist intentional communities. Under his leadership, the community of Modern Times, New York lasted several years with thousands of residents without maintaining a police force or court system.

Modern Times was also unique in that it did not end in failure as many homesteads did, but instead was swallowed up by the growing United States. Warren espoused a philosophy based on what he called *The Sovereignty of the Individual*, a principle which recognized the value in individualism and stressed the need for mutual respect of other free individuals' right to be free from coercion. He stressed that individuals living in a complex society have interlocking interests and as such, there will be conflicts and there will have to be compromises. Warren was adamant that free people should not impose their will on others and instead allow diversity to reign.

According to Warren, *"Liberty, then, is the sovereignty of the individual, and never shall man know liberty until each and every individual is acknowledged to be the only legitimate sovereign of his or her person, time, and property, each living and acting at his own cost; and not until we live in a society where each can exercise his right of sovereignty at all times without clashing with or violating that of others."*

With this principle in mind, let us examine a few scenarios involving conflicting views of property and see if there is a possibility for coexistence. These scenarios represent some of the common objections and most difficult questions to answer.

First, imagine the state has dissolved and people are free to organize and homestead without intervention. In the absence of the state, competing insurance companies would insure people's property against theft or harm. Now, Imagine we have two adjacent plots of land, plot A and plot B. Plot A is occupied by a farmer, his house, and his crops, all of which he acquired through his own labor. The farmer on plot A supports private ownership of property. Plot B is unoccupied. However, prior to the state's collapse the land had been sold to someone who owned the title but never actually homesteaded or made changes to the land.

One day, a group of anarcho-communists discover the two plots of land and decide to homestead plot B. The AnComs begin planting crops, building shelters, and altering the lay of the land. The farmer from plot A is friends with the man who holds the title to plot B so he decides to question the AnComs about their new settlement. The AnComs insist that it's obvious no one has lived on or made use of the land and declare themselves the rightful stewards. The farmer says the title holder to plot B will not be making use of the land. Is it legitimate for the AnComs to occupy and homestead plot B?

If the previous owner has no plans to return to dispute and it is clear that no one's sovereignty will be violated in the process, we believe plot B could be homesteaded without the need for conflict. Also, if the title holder to plot B came into possession of the land with the assistance of any state privilege then it was not justly acquired and therefore not a legitimate claim. To satisfy this argument one would need to make reasonable effort to determine whether the property in question was in use. This leads us to a major issue with deciding land claims of this nature: the arguments tend to venture into arbitrary territory which makes it difficult to establish norms. For example, how long must one wait before homesteading someone else's unused property? And what qualifies as unused? Also, who decides how much land is "too much" for one person? How do we answer these questions while respecting the sovereignty of each individual?

We think this is an important time to reiterate the need for spontaneous order and discretion based on mutual respect. What we mean is that in a truly free society without imposed central authority there is no way to force or coerce every single person to live according to the property norms of your choosing. The vast human experience guarantees that we are not always going to agree on complex moral issues, and with that being the case, it is best to find a way to handle these issues without hurting people or throwing them in cages. Of course, there will be rare occasions where violent and unreasonable people will need to be subdued or isolated, but that would be the exception to the rule in a world where people are attempting to avoid the use of oppressive tactics seen throughout history.

We imagine a world where some communities implement private property norms and others have property arrangements that resemble unowned or community ownership. How will each and every conflict play out with such a patchwork of norms? Only the individuals involved in each particular situation can decide. Unless AnComs and AnCaps are prepared to yield the force of the state to ensure their specific property views are the new monopoly, we better get used to mutual respect and compromise. A one size fits all solution is already a part of the problem we face today.

Let's look at one more example to see how these conflicts might be resolved. What happens if the title holder to plot B returns to find the AnComs living on his land? The title holder tells the AnComs he has been waiting for the right time before he chose to build on the land. The AnComs say that they found the land unused and believe they now have a stronger claim due to homesteading. Who has the stronger claim? How do we resolve this conflict without resorting to violence? Many anarchist thinkers have suggested competing arbitration agencies which would be responsible for sorting out conflicts. If the original title holder calls his insurance agency (IA1) to defend his claim to the land, the AnComs would likely hire insurance agency 2 (IA2) to defend their claim. The two agencies would consider the claims and attempt to resolve the conflict as impartial third parties. In the event that the two agencies cannot resolve the conflict to the satisfaction of their customers, the title holder and AnComs would hire an arbitration agency to settle the dispute for good. If after consulting with the insurance agency, and the arbitration agency, one of the parties are still not satisfied, a private protection agency could be hired to enforce the ruling. Obviously, this increases the possibility of conflict, but in the end we believe the lack of incentives for war will deter individuals from pursuing this path. Especially, as humanity grows to accept the sovereignty of each individual. Insurance agencies will be influenced by market demand to resolve these situations as peacefully as possible because their business will be negatively impacted by stories of violence, especially in the age of livestream and YouTube.

Again, we stress that the above situations are entirely theoretical. We have no way of knowing how free people will choose to self-organize and handle dispute resolution. There will always be conflicts and differences of opinion. It is up to each of us to hold ourselves to a higher standard and strive to always respect the sovereignty of other individuals and use our best discretion in each case of conflict. Even if the whole of society is forced to accept one specific dogma there will always be dissenters and the only way to stop the dissent is to enact totalitarian control. We can either have freedom to disagree and peacefully resolve conflicts, or we can continue the cycle of violence and coercion. It has been said that ideas which are worthy do not require force or violence to implement. If one stands by their beliefs wholeheartedly they should be able to respectfully debate the merits and potential failures without resorting to violence.

The Revolutionary Potential of "Illegal" Immigrants

We are going to take a look at one more area of conflict among students of radical political philosophy. After examining differences of opinion on property and the environment we believe it is essential to discuss the arguments around borders and immigration. We start by considering several key questions. What would migration look like in the absence of the state? How does a society's view on property affect the view of immigration? Would there still be a class of people known as "illegals"?

Traditionally, libertarian and anarchist positions on borders have favored an "open border" solution. This would be in contrast to a "closed border" with immigration controls. This is naturally in line with anarchism considering the fact that governments implement and control borders, and anarchists seek to abolish governments. However, recently some anarcho-capitalists and libertarians have argued for closed borders. They believe private property norms justify forcibly restricting the movement of other free humans, even beyond the borders of their own property. The Alt-Right takes it a step further and argues that the State may even be a necessary evil in order to save "western civilization" and "traditional values" from an "invasion" of immigrants.

The discussion on borders often centers around whether or not immigrants will have access to "public property" while visiting. Closed border advocates argue that in a stateless society based on private property norms, immigrants would not be welcome unless they were explicitly invited or had employment opportunities. If the immigrant is not invited or does not have a contractual agreement they would not be allowed to occupy private property. Since the closed border/ private property advocates believe there will be no such thing as "public property" in a free society they argue that immigrants without an invitation will have nowhere to go and will thus be trespassing and subject to physical removal. We argue that in the absence of the state, land currently known as "public property" (or land controlled by the government) would revert back to unowned property. This would allow for individuals to travel across or homestead on this previously government held land. Those who argue that taxpayers should have the first claim to this land ignore the

80

reality that failing to join the counter-economy and continuing to fund the state is not a noble act. Taxpayers and agorists are equally enslaved under the statist system, but when the state collapses, favors will not be paid to those who extended the life of the state by failing to withdraw financial support. We find it laughable that "anarchists" would suggest that paying taxes is honorable and deserving of special privileges in the post-state world. Sure, we are all forced to pay taxes under the threat of violence, and the fact that people pay under duress should not be held against them, but at the same time, those who have the courage to take the risk certainly deserve an extra level of respect and admiration.

One major roadblock in the borders debate is the use of faulty terminology. A valid objection to the concept of public property is the association of the concept with government controlled property. However, we do not think public property needs to be exclusively thought of as government property. In his essay *In Defense of Public Space,* libertarian thinker Roderick T. Long discusses the problems with the public and private debate:

"When we think of public property, we think of government property. But this has not traditionally been the case. Throughout history, legal doctrine has recognized, alongside property owned by the organized public (that is, the public as organized into a state and represented by government officials), an additional category of property owned by the unorganized public. This was property that the public at large was deemed to have a right of access to, but without any presumption that government would be involved in the matter at all.

I have no interest in defending public property in the sense of property belonging to the organized public (i.e., the state). In fact, I do not think government property is public property at all; it is really the private property of an agency calling itself the government. What I wish to defend is the idea of property rights inherent in the unorganized public."

It seems as if the time has come to abandon terms like open and closed borders in favor of decentralized borders. We imagine a free society with decentralized borders would consist of a mixture of open borders, closed borders, public property, private property and unowned land. We believe a network of competing public and private spaces which allow for freedom of movement is most consistent with the sovereignty of the individual.

Regardless of theoretical concerns, government borders are a utopian idea to begin with, especially when considering areas as large as Europe and the United States. In most of the world (and especially in Western countries), governments can't even secure their own prisons and airports, which increasingly resemble fortresses. Furthermore, creating an effective and staffed wall for the border of the U.S. is barely even physically or financially possible. Over the course of a three-year project, the U.S. government spent $2.4 billion to build 670 miles of very unimpressive fencing along the Mexican border. Considering the U.S. shares roughly 6,000 miles of international borders, it would cost $19 billion to construct a small, unimpressive fence along that entire border. This figure does not include the cost of staffing the fence, or the costs that would come along with making a fence large enough, the barbed wires, weapons, and a buffer zone. These additional expenses could easily double or triple the cost of the project.

Not to mention this militarized border would require an expansion of the already bloated police and surveillance states. Currently, most of the U.S. border is not even fenced or staffed with military, and there has been no major disaster as a result. Some would argue the violence along borders, particularly the southern border between the U.S. and Mexico, is an example of a major disaster that could be remedied with tighter border controls. However, it is the state and the insistence on intervening in free humans movement and exchange of goods which fuels the cartels and gangs that cluster around distribution points along the border. The blame should be placed on the restriction of movement that comes along with closed borders, not a lack of border control. Even if a massive wall were built and soldiers were staffed every few feet, the closed border would create a demand for immigration, and thus a huge financial incentive for soldiers and government workers to use their positions to smuggle people inside. This is exactly why drugs and contraband flow through prisons, behind many layers of walls and barbed wire. Even at airports, which are now as secure as prisons, people are still capable of sneaking guns and other prohibited items onto flights.

Some of the fascists formerly masquerading as anarchists argue that allowing open borders will lead to a flood of foreigners who lack an understanding of the cultural norms of the nation-state. Even if we are to ignore the fact that the nation-state is a fictitious creation, we should not stray from principle based on fears and assumptions about the future. These proponents of closed borders argue against immigration because they believe the migrants will vote for statism and the welfare state. If these migrants are allowed to enter we will see statism grow and libertarianism die, they argue. These pro-border "libertarians" are effectively calling for pre-crime laws and profiling in the name of protecting borders, which is a blatant contradiction of libertarian values. Ironically enough, many of the modern libertarians that advocate for closed borders belong to the Ludwig Von Mises institute, an academic institution dedicated to continuing the legacy of Ludwig Von Mises, the founder of Austrian economics. Mises was a Jewish refugee during World War 2 and would have likely been killed by closed-borders policies.

Just as the statists will argue in favor of a surveillance state to prevent terrorism, the border-thumper will try to ban movement in the name of saving "Western Civilization". Whether the argument for a closed border is coming from the left or the right, it is based on the worldview of central planners who do not have faith in the power of individuals to self-organize.

Our final suggestion on the topic of immigration and borders may sound like heresy to some, but we believe it offers the only possibility of creating harmony among free people and thus, furthering our opportunities for a world without a state. Conversation. Conversation and compassionate communication are needed on the part of both the local population and the migrants. Even in the state controlled world we have today we should oppose granting the state power over border control. Opponents of open borders are so adamant that immigrants from non-Western nations (i.e., those with predominantly brown skin) are going to be statists, leftists, or leeches of the welfare state, that they are willing to support the state to enforce borders. They refuse to search for common ground with their brothers and sisters who happen to be born on a different piece of land.

As anarchists, we should oppose closed and State controlled borders. As agorists, we should strive to form alliances with immigrants and teach them the value of remaining unregistered by the state and operating in the counter-economy. For an example of the potential for converting "illegal" immigrants to revolutionary agorists let's reexamine Peru's informal economy as mentioned in chapter 2. In *The Other Path*, Hernando De Soto notes that in the 1970's Peru's rural population began flooding into the cities. The migrants moved en masse from the countryside to the cities, causing the migrant population in Lima, Peru to explode from 300,000 to 1.9 million between 1940 and 1981. The migrants left the countryside to escape poor living conditions and in search of financial opportunities in the big cities. Upon arriving, the migrants were greeted with hostility from people within the borders of their own nation.

De Soto notes that *"the greatest hostility the migrants encountered was from the legal system"*. The barriers the migrants faced within the cities seemed to be a result of statism and interference in the market, but also policies aimed at discriminating against the rural, indigenous populations of Peru. *"Quite simply, Peru's legal institutions had been developed over the years to meet the needs and bolster the privileges of certain dominant groups in the cities and to isolate the peasants geographically in rural areas,"* De Soto writes. Ultimately, the formerly rural population recognized that the legal system was designed to exclude them and *"discovered that they must compete not only against people but also against the system"*.

It is this reality of state-enforced barriers to entry in the marketplace that drove the migrants to join the "informal economy". They chose to purposefully and voluntarily break the law in pursuit of financial gain and a better standard of living. Imagine if a collection of Freedom Cells dedicated themselves to welcoming and allying with incoming "illegal" immigrants in an effort to help them understand the value of the informal or counter-economy. This "Agorist Welcoming Committee" could help connect immigrants to an underground network of black and

84

grey market services, including access to community healthcare and untaxed employment. By choosing to relinquish fear-driven xenophobia, the *Conscious Agorist Movement* could create a cadre of self-aware immigrant agorists capable of wielding their collective economic power. Individuals are unpredictable, and there is no telling how people are going to act or behave once they move someplace new. Perhaps this fear of the unknown is what pushes many to make assumptions about strangers. Regardless, we have the power to influence newcomers in our communities, and in the case of immigrants, they are prone to favor counter-economic activity since there are so many legal restrictions preventing them from entering the statist economy. The revolution is in the conversations and we should seize every opportunity to organize with immigrants to overthrow statist, authoritarian borders.

Part 3: Creating Conscious Agoras

The goal of this final part of the Manifesto of the Free Humans pertains to both of our specific preferences for a Conscious Agora existing in a stateless society. It is important to remember that we do not believe in one size fits all models, and are not attempting to state that every free, conscious agora should organize in the fashion described in the following pages. Obviously, our subjective preferences are contained in these chapters, but we see our ideal intentional community as existing among the myriad of diverse, unique communities that will exist in a truly freed marketplace of ideas. We encourage the reader to take our words and review them and compare to your own values and principles. Do our ideas measure up to your vision? If not, please take what you can learn from our efforts and adapt it to your community's specific needs.

We believe in freedom and thus we believe in diversity. Our vision of an intentional community will be one among the many coexisting communities, microstates, communes, neighborhoods, and other yet-to-be discovered ways of self-organizing. The actual formation of such a community is slated to begin in early 2020. We will spend the next four years building towards this goal via the Freedom Cell movement. While the political system continues to disappoint the masses, Freedom Cells and agorism offer a bright future.

The next three chapters explain the Points of Unity for this coming intentional community: Sovereignty of the Individual, PermAgora, and Mindfulness. The triangle on the following page represents the culmination of these three principles. When combined with a counter-economic strategy these principles lead to the realization of the Conscious Agora.

<u>Sovereignty of the Individual</u>

When imagining our ideal community, there are several considerations to make. As we have discussed, there is a vast spectrum of opinions regarding property, the environment, immigration, and the organizational structure society will take. No matter the agenda item, our first question is always: *does the action impede upon another free persons right to live free from coercion and violence?* Those in favor of animal equality could also expand the question to ask, do my actions prevent *any life* from living free of coercion and violence?

Whichever principle you start with, the goal is the reduction of violence and oppression in our everyday lives. This is a foundational principle for the establishment of a Conscious Agora. As mentioned earlier, this principle is known as the *sovereignty of the individual* and was first expounded by Josiah Warren in the 1840's. In his book *Partisans of Freedom: A Study in American Anarchism*, William O. Reichert describes Warren as the "chief architect of libertarianism." Despite his best efforts, many modern anarchists are oblivious to his powerful body of work.

Warren wholeheartedly believed that any action taken to limit the rights of the individual was immoral and would lead to strife. In his *Manifesto* he writes:

"The forming of societies or any other artificial combinations IS the first, greatest, and most fatal mistake ever committed by legislators and by reformers. That all these combinations require the surrender of the natural sovereignty of the INDIVIDUAL over her or his person, time, property and responsibilities, to the government of the combination. That this tends to prostrate the individual--To reduce him to a mere piece of a machine; involving others in responsibility for his acts, and being involved in responsibilities for the acts and sentiments of his associates; he lives & acts, without proper control over his own affairs, without certainty as to the results of his actions, and almost without brains that he dares to use on his own account; and consequently never realizes the great objects for which society is professedly formed."

Warren came to these conclusions after his experiences with Robert Owen, a British social reform activist who had launched a utopian community in Scotland before coming to America to launch another community in New Harmony, Indiana. Warren was living in Cincinnati, Ohio until he decided move his whole family to New Harmony to join Owen's community. The decision would greatly affect his philosophical path. Warren would later note that New Harmony failed due to the decision to put communal interests above that of each individual. With his newfound appreciation for individuality, Warren left New Harmony in 1927 and headed back to Cincinnati to further develop his theories. In 1847, Warren established a community known as Utopia just thirty miles from Cincinnati. Finally, in 1850, Warren went to New York and established Modern Times on Long Island. The community was successful for several years under the direction of Josiah Warren and his theories. Eventually, Modern Times would evolve into the city known as Brentwood. The town was described as a thriving community with a printing plant, a carriage factory, and a furniture factory. A place where every house had a garden, every person was free to live as they pleased, and there were no police, courts, jails, or even a single recorded crime. Residents reported that conflicts were handled by isolating or refusing to do business with those who chose to violate the sovereignty of other individuals.

All of this was made possible because Josiah Warren founded the community on the basic understanding that every individual's right to self-ownership would be respected. *"The great principle of human elevation was perceived to be the SOVEREIGNTY OF EVERY INDIVIDUAL over his or her Person and Time and Property and Responsibilities"*, Warren wrote. He also believed that only through a process called "Disconnection" could an individual untangle their connections to other human beings and truly respect the sovereignty of the individual. Warren extended his individualist vision to economics, stating that a version of the Labor Theory of Value, or what he called Equitable Commerce, ensured that unequal exchanges did not take place. In this way, Warren can be seen as the earliest proponent of mutualist economics. Although we favor the subjective theory of value, we appreciate Josiah Warren's development of concepts like Time Banking and Labor Hours, which he arrived at through his Equitable Commerce theory. Ultimately, we completely accept the sovereignty of every individual to organize their economic transactions how they please, regardless of our own personal preferences.

It is Warren's Sovereignty of the Individual that will guide the intentional community we plan to establish. This will require purchasing land and, unfortunately, paying property taxes. Of course, agorists should always strive to opt out of taxation. However, in the current political climate it seems inevitable that free humans will be best served with a piece of land with which to build for the future and propagate the message of freedom. By purchasing land before the state collapses or is defeated, we hope to be proactive in our efforts to build the counter-economy and the coming agora. It has become increasingly difficult to sit by and live among "mainstream" society, all the while contributing to unsustainable systems that do not serve to harmonize relationships between the inhabitants of this planet.

The hope is that we are able to gain a foothold on a piece of land and continue to propagate the agorist message until the state becomes weak enough (and the agora strong enough) that our community decides we are no longer under threat to pay property taxes, a strategy we will explore in detail later in this section. The freedom of land also allows a Freedom Cell to grow their own food, cultivate independence via counter-economic activity, and maintain a level of privacy from governments and their loyalists. A Freedom Cell could use the land to build community centers for hosting meet-ups, counter-economic markets, radical music festivals, skill shares, and cell building.

Within this free agora each member of the Freedom Cell will be free to make a living as they please (provided they respect individual sovereignty), use any currency they choose, grow what food they want, and build whatever home they choose. Obviously, a community can decide to only permit vegans, for example, or allow only sustainable methods of building to be used, but each individual entering into the community will be made fully aware of any contractual obligations that may exist. Our main goal is to establish that every single person choosing to live within the walls of our community is free to do as they please, provided they are not harming anyone else. The intentional community that will begin in 2020 only has two other stipulations for potential community members, both of which make up the remaining corners of our triangle.

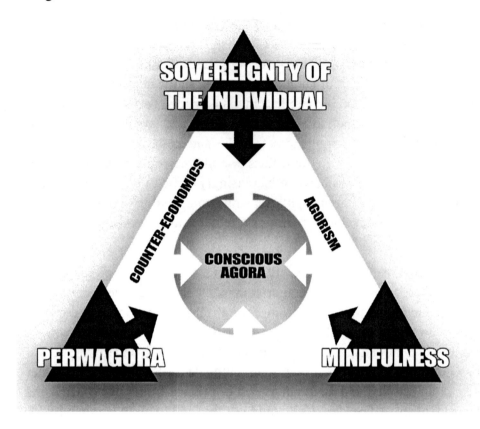

PermAgora

A key aspect of The Conscious Resistance is that humanity needs to reevaluate the nature of our interpersonal relationships and connections. Not only when it comes to each other, but our relationship with animals and the planet itself. The morality of our relationship with the planet and animals should be reviewed, and in fact, must be reviewed if we want to survive with any type of prosperity. If the goal is consistency, we must take the time to examine and challenge every one of our preconceived notions of the world. Ultimately, this comes down to an individual choosing to review and adjust their own behaviors and actions, not only in relation to taxation and voting, but every single one of our daily habits which are not aligned with our principles.

When imagining our ideal community we do not envision a place where the land is exploited, polluted, and stripped of the finite resources located within the Earth. We have no intention of living in a community where the Earth is viewed as an object to dominate, a means to an end, or a backdrop to our consumerist lifestyles. Refusing to initiate violence in our relationships should extend to all our relationships, including the relationship with this planet. These realizations led us to the next corner of the triangle: *PermAgora*, or sustainability. We wish to create an intentional community that honors the sovereignty of every individual to be free to make their own choices provided they harm no other. In our community, this would extend to our philosophy on the environment. This means that any permanent resident or visitor to this community would be voluntarily choosing to live in harmony with the environment and community at large. We are not interested in forcing other free humans outside our community to live as we choose in this ideal intentional community. Instead, we hope to live as an example of what is possible when conscious individuals choose to change their own behavior without the need for threats from the state or other forms of coercion.

A great example of living a low-impact lifestyle without the force of law is environmental activist and adventurist Rob Greenfield. He is known for taking on extreme adventures in order to highlight environmental damage and waste. Greenfield has taken several bicycle tours across the U.S., dumpster diving in every city and small town he stopped in. Greenfield estimates that he has dumpster dived in over 2,000 dumpsters in over 25 states. In 2016, he launched his "Trash Me" project which saw him spend a month wearing all of the trash he created. Using a special suit he walked around for 30 days with bags of trash attached to him. All of this was done to raise awareness about important aspects of the fight for a healthier species and planet. The best part of all? Greenfield is not out there calling for government intervention. He recognizes that the only way to heal the planet is through individual awareness and action. Hopefully, with the help of people like Rob, we can help inspire our species to action before our time on this planet expires.

Within our intentional community, sustainable practices will be employed in the process of building shelter, growing food, and working with animals. Sustainable means using technologies and practices that do not deplete resources and create as little waste as possible. We imagine a community living in harmony with the environment and leading low-impact lifestyles. Some activists have also begun calling for "regenerative" practices that not only sustain the environment, but regenerate the soil and return it to its naturally healthy state. In this way, "Regenerative Activism" might be thought of as taking actions that sustain and regenerate the health of the individual, as well as the community at large. When we began researching sustainable practices and experimenting with urban farming we consistently found references to Permaculture.

Permaculture is portmanteau of permanent agriculture and culture. It refers to an approach to designing communities and perennial agricultural systems based on relationships found in nature. It has also expanded into a philosophy on how we interact with the world. Permaculture systems have the potential to be far more productive and much less energy intensive than conventional agriculture. Permaculture was first developed by Austrian farmer Sepp Holzer on his own farm in the early 1960's and then further theoretically developed by Australians Bill Mollison and David Holmgren during the 1970's. Essential to Permaculture is the idea that agricultural systems should not require a lot of work to maintain, they should improve the land, and produce in ways that provide for humans, animals, and other local ecosystems.

There are three ethics central to Permaculture philosophy: earth care, people care, and fair share. Earth care means to rebuild the natural capital of the environment and to take care of the soil. People care simply means caring for family, community companionship, and self. This also involves self-reliance and working to reduce the production and consumption of unnecessary material resources. Fair share means to voluntarily set limits on consumption and redistribute the surplus back into the community. This is not a call for centralized management of resources, but instead a recognition of the need for self-organizing among sovereign individuals. In a truly freed market individuals will prefer to do business with communities operating with sustainability and environmental awareness in mind. Those who practice unsustainable practices and environmental destruction will quickly lose support and economic power.

In his book, *Permaculture: Principles and Pathways beyond Sustainability,* David Holmgren expanded on the Permaculture philosophy with the addition of 12 principles. We will not be examining each principle individually, however, they are provided to emphasize the mentality behind the philosophy of Permaculture.

1. Observe and Interact

2. Catch and Store Energy

3. Obtain a Yield

4. Apply Self Regulation and Accept Feedback

5. Use and Value Renewable Resources and Services

6. Produce No Waste

7. Design From Patterns to Details

8. Integrate Rather Than Segregate

9. Use Small and Slow Solutions

10. Use and Value Diversity

11. Use Edges and Value the Marginal

12. Creatively Use and Respond to Change

Permaculture can be viewed as a less forceful, more mindful, approach to living off the land. Agorism is also a less forceful, mindful approach applied to economics and exchange. Both philosophies encourage creation and building. When combined together we get *PermAgora*, the synthesis of permaculture and agorism and the application of both approaches simultaneously. PermAgora is a developing school of thought based on the research of permaculture student Eric McCool. In Eric's words, *"the goal is the restoration of the natural systems of the planet, and changes in our way of life so that we need not be dominated by violence and coercion."* To remove the violence and coercion from every aspect of our lives we must adopt new ways of thinking about the environment. The coming Conscious Agora will benefit from an alliance of Freedom Cells practicing PermAgora. We hope to lead the way.

Strong Hearts and Revolutionary Minds

The next essential piece of the triangle of liberation is the concept of "Mindfulness". This simple concept could be also be termed "mindful awareness" or simply, awareness. Mindfulness represents the reality that we must apply a sense of heightened awareness, a constantly self-aware state of mind, to every one of our actions if we hope to continue the spiritual evolution of our species. Throughout The Conscious Resistance series, we have stressed that achieving peace and freedom is a task that requires more than just knowledge or logic. Compassion and communication skills are also essential if one is attempting to create positive change in the world. In past generations, people on different ends of political and religious spectrums have seen each other as mortal enemies. This behavior has negatively impacted living standards on all sides (except those ruling from above). When groups with divergent views are able to set aside their differences, the standard of living is typically elevated on all sides. When groups are locked in endless war or conflict everyone suffers, except, once again, those ruling from above. Oftentimes, feuds and conflicts continue due to manipulation from the establishment. Sometimes, these disputes are simply the result of inflated egos on both sides. In many cases, people seem more concerned with being right than finding solutions. It is this mentality that we are working to heal.

The term "The Conscious Resistance" was born out of an awareness that the world is in a state of imbalance due to the influence of small groups of elitists working to use the state and corporate power to live off the fruits of the rest of the world. It was also born from our individual realization that those who wish to control and manipulate others do so because of their own pain. That pain is absorbed by the population and then turned into fear and anger. This results in states of anxiety and disharmony which allows for the continued manipulation at the hands of the same fearful elite. Our ambition is to lead the way by being open and vulnerable about our own struggles and triumphs. For the two of us this means incorporating meditation, positive affirmations, visualization, and other practices into our message of anarchism. Because of this decision to focus on healing and interpersonal relationships, The Conscious Resistance could also be referred to as *Holistic Anarchism*.

The term holistic is related to the theory known as Holism, which argues that *"the universe and nature should be viewed in terms of interacting wholes (as of living organisms) that are more than the mere sum of elementary particles"*. Holistic is defined as *"relating to or concerned with wholes or with complete systems rather than with the analysis of, treatment of, or dissection into parts"*. For example, holistic medicine typically treats body and mind while holistic ecology examines humans and the environment as a single system. Holistic anarchism posits that the end of statism and authoritarianism will not come by examination of political and economic theory alone. The fight against the state should be viewed holistically, meaning we should view the problem in terms of the whole system. This means reflecting on all the forms of oppression faced by the free people of our world. This also means being honest about the ways our personal habits and prejudices are contributing to the oppression we see. By understanding the fight against the state as a battle with many arenas, and choosing to reflect on the steps we can take as individuals, we are employing holistic anarchism. Ultimately, it is not just the tyrants in office, or the theft of taxation that is keeping us from being free. It is our own self-limiting thoughts and actions which truly hold us back.

In *Finding Freedom In An Age Of Confusion*, we explored the concept of Nonviolent Communication (NVC), a conflict resolution technique that was promoted by activist and psychologist Marshall Rosenberg. The premise of NVC is simple: instead of arguing about who is right or wrong, and who must win or lose, people should strive to have win-win interactions by focusing on ensuring that the needs of each person are met. The goal is to find solutions to problems by addressing the unmet needs of everyone in the equation. Again, from a holistic anarchist perspective the way we communicate with other free people is equally important to making sure our arguments are sound. It's extremely difficult to have a rational discussion when both parties feel their concerns are not being heard. Such a battle of insecurities is not likely to lead to a better understanding of one another. How can we ever hope to possibly influence others if they choose to communicate with anger, aggression, or impatience? We recognize that human connection is essential on the path to liberty. We lead by example and learn to communicate without violence, condescension, or passive aggressive tendencies.

Daryl Davis is a shining example of how the power of love, understanding and compassion can overcome the darkness of hate and bigotry. Davis, a black, 58-year-old blues musician and author, has managed to successfully convince hundreds of racists to quit the KKK. Davis goes deep behind enemy lines to Klan rallies and white supremacist meetings and attempts to make friends with people who hate him. Davis says he has been doing it for over 30 years. He is even responsible for single-handedly causing the entire Maryland chapter of the KKK to dissolve. Years ago, Davis began seeking out members of the KKK so he could learn more about racism first hand. In the beginning, his initial goal was just to try to gain some type of understanding of why these people choose to be racist. On at least two separate occasions has had to defend himself from violent Klan members. Most often though, these meetings happen without any incident. While there are plenty of tense moments, the interactions between Davis and the racists he encounters are surprisingly pleasant. Instead of focusing heavily on race and areas of disagreement, Davis instead tries to focus on areas of agreement and steers the conversation towards common ground.

"If you spend just five minutes with your arch enemy, you will discover that you have something in common, and if you spend ten minutes, you'll find you have something else in common," he says.

Davis has a closet filled with Klansman uniforms, all of them given to him by friends and former Klansman who quit the racist cult as a result of their friendship. One KKK member and Baltimore City Police officer even gave Davis both his Klansman uniform and his police officer's uniform. The approach that Davis has taken in converting racists into friends is the same approach that anarchists can use to turn statists into free thinking human beings.

One such anarchist attempting to find common ground is Sterlin Luxan. Rather than holistic or conscious anarchism, he refers to his approach as "relationalism" or relational anarchism. Luxan, also known as the "Psychologic Anarchist", is a professional writer, editor, research assistant, and aspiring counseling psychologist with a BA in psychology. In his essay *Anarchy and Emotion Pt. 2*, Luxan explains his viewpoint:

"I call it relationalism. It is the philosophy that promotes absence of rulers and total freedom through relationships and social healing, rather than through the traditional routes of argumentation, persuasion, or economic theorizing. Current conceptions of anarchism have been hyper focused on the LEM Axis. That is, they are geared toward solving Logical, Economic, and Moral problems of society and government."

Instead, Luxan suggests employing empathy when dealing with others.

"If people are attuned to each others' feelings, there is less of an opportunity for violence and aggression to erupt. This is the application of the therapeutic alliance to society-at-large for building a freer, more psychologically stable world. In order to build a social order based on logical, moral, or economic truths, humans must first grapple with their emotional worlds and how they relate and interact with all people. They must learn to heal each other through being together and uniting, in much the same way that a counselor helps a client get better through their mutually agreed upon alliance. In this sense, the philosophy of relationalism sees the anarchist as a social healer that creates communities and nurtures love."

Luxan's relationalism is perfectly aligned with our message of holistic anarchism. We applaud his efforts to explore the intersection of anarchism and psychology, in the same way we have explored anarchism and spirituality. Our hope is that the message of freedom and empowerment will continue to grow until there exist anarchists in a variety of fields of research, each pushing for true freedom through the filter of their particular area of expertise.

The evolution of consciousness is absolutely necessary for true, lasting freedom to be achieved. We boldly stand by our positions and arguments made in this series, but the reality is that none of the solutions presented will succeed if the broken and confused people of this world refuse to do the necessary internal work for individual healing to transpire. The insecurities, doubts, and fears will differ person to person, so an honest self-examination is needed to decipher where to begin your healing process. If we want to heal the deeper root causes which allow violence to be perpetuated among our species we must be willing to face ourselves. If we fail to recognize healing and personal growth as a vital part of the fight for a more free, ethical world we are setting ourselves up for failure. Our only hope in creating a free society based on mutual aid, voluntary association, and individual sovereignty is to embark upon a path of mindfulness, reflection, forgiveness, acceptance, healing, empowerment, and finally, self-actualization. These seven steps are the ongoing path towards The Conscious Resistance.

Mobility vs. Homesteading

It is a wonderful experience to witness the beautiful expressions of diversity that spring forth as individuals pursue their own version of freedom. After all, freedom is a personal and individual experience. There is no one size fits all model or path to freedom; the outcome depends on individual preferences and circumstance. This principle holds true with the agorist lifestyle and engaging in counter-economics. Although we are describing what an intentional community may look like from our perspective, some freedom seekers view mobility as the ultimate expression of freedom and may choose to live nomadic lifestyles. Others may choose to opt out of community or neighborhood living and live the life of a hermit. All of these paths are valid and compatible with agorism.

When creating the ideal living situation, many variables must be taken into consideration. *Where do you want to live? How many people will live with you? What kind of community do you want? Where will you get your food? How will you make an income or provide for basic necessities?*

For some individuals, organizing into Freedom Cells will naturally lead to forming communities and communal living. Some will choose to live in the same neighborhoods or towns, as in the Texas Freedom Grounds, and others will choose to share land. But what of those who say they don't want to live one place? What about the restless travelers and the noble nomads who would rather live life on the road? Is there a better opportunity to realize freedom in your life and the life of your family by choosing to live nowhere and everywhere?

One of the main reasons we argue for establishing a community with land to tend and defend is the ability to grow your own food and produce your own goods. Growing your own food is a huge step towards independence. Although some creative folks have engineered ways to grow food on top of vehicles, it is extremely difficult to sustain yourself this way. Also, having a piece of land allows for the building of shelters and structures which can store supplies, food, and everything you need to survive an emergency. Granted, one could simply rent out a storage space and keep all these items stored until needed, but what happens when the shit hits the fan and you are on the road, thousands of miles away from your survival supplies?

We believe it is essential for Freedom Cells to begin thinking about having a location to rendezvous in the event of an emergency. If you live in the city, this might include two places; one within the city as a meeting point, and another meeting place outside of the city limits, ideally on a piece of land where you have supplies waiting. If you find yourself on the road during an emergency, you may have trouble finding a safe place to stay and supplies to sustain you. Hopefully we will soon have a large Freedom Cell Network across the globe that will ensure none of our brothers and sisters go without help. On the other hand, if you and your family are living in a bus, RV, or simply towing your tiny house everywhere you go, you have a certain level of freedom that landowners do not. Two great examples of nomadic anarchist families are the Blushes in Austin, Texas and The Undocumented Humans in Arizona. Most of the families and individuals we know who are living the nomadic life say they enjoy a level of freedom they did not know while paying rent on land, houses, or apartments. There may be times when an emergency requires bugging out of your house or land. The ability to have your house and your vehicle in one machine is definitely a benefit in this situation. Nomads with vehicles will likely have most of their important possessions with them, and will not be faced with the difficult choice of what to take and what to leave behind.

Some free people will prefer solitary travel, either in their vehicles or as hitch-hiking adventurers living off the counter-economy. Others will want to be more secluded and choose to homestead land in the wilderness, far away from other homes and communities. Perhaps this person prefers the independence of seclusion, or they have social anxiety or other issues that make a rural lifestyle preferable. Although the hermits might not be directly connected to a community by physical proximity, they can be connected digitally through FreedomCells.org or other online groups that allow for organizing and exchanging with other freedom-minded individuals.

Whether your path finds you hiding out in caves, sailing on the freedom fleet, nomading on the bus, relaxing in the neighborhood, or living in a community of thousands, the goal is freedom. No matter what living situation you choose there are dozens of methods to participate in the counter-economy. Our preferred place of residence should not prevent us from establishing a powerful alliance of interconnected and interlocking Freedom Cells and free communities.

Getting Off The Control Grid and Defending The Agora

When discussing the idea of a free society, one of the most frequently asked questions is *"how do we get from here to there?"*. The transition is without a doubt the most challenging step on the path to freedom, but throughout this book we have laid the foundation for a possible future. Now, we will end this journey by exploring how we can sever our involuntary relationship with the state, once and for all. Our goal is to establish alternative ways of living prior to our emancipation from government. These alternatives are the lifeboats that will allow us to escape the sinking ship. This is where the importance of Freedom Cells, counter-economics and competing with state services and institutions comes into play.

As free thinking people begin to create free communities in geographical regions that are still disputed or claimed by governments, there will be a need for self-defense. Some free humans will also want to agitate the existing government in hopes of weakening it and spurring on its demise. Our primary focus should be on growing the counter-economy and agora and we do this by reducing our dependence and support of the existing government. We need a sustained, coordinated campaign of noncooperation, tax resistance, counter-economic activity, and mass opting out of the structures operated by state and corporate power. This should be done in tandem with a push for individual healing, community building, and compassionate activism.

We believe tax resistance is absolutely necessary to weaken the state. Those invested in the counter-economy are already taking sales tax away from the state and if you can make your money "off the books" or "under the table" do not hesitate. If you can be paid in alternative currencies even better. Every cent you take from the state is a victory on the path to realizing the Conscious Agora. Some Freedom Cells may choose to continue to pay their taxes, or avoid the income tax and sales tax when possible, until the time arrives where the state is too weak to pursue them or they are capable of defending themselves from thieving tax collectors. Connected cells and communities may choose to band together to coordinate an organized tax resistance campaign to further agitate and weaken the state.

If we work diligently we can make a coordinated tax resistance campaign go viral across Freedom Cells spread throughout the U.S. If we are able to prevent the state from taking funds that equal the annual defense budget we believe the state will take notice of their waning influence and power.

The U.S. government's revenue from federal, state, and local sources was estimated to be $7 trillion during 2016. About $4.6 trillion of that comes from income and payroll taxes, the exact taxes one avoids by joining the counter-economy. During 2016, the Department of Defense (responsible for the U.S. military) had a budget of $582 billion. As the numbers show, it would only require a loss of less than one trillion dollars in income and payroll taxes to remove the budget for the Department of Defense. This would make it difficult (not impossible) for the state to continue to wage war and it would send a message that the people are getting organized. The state will be forced to have the Federal Reserve print massive sums of money which will only hasten the push towards hyper-inflation and economic chaos. Amidst this chaos, the agorists will jump into action and offer counter-economic services and assistance to those who chose not to prepare. The state could also take money away from popular government services like welfare, veteran assistance, etc. and redirect it towards the war effort but this is also likely to be an unpopular move. Will the people really stand by and do nothing as their government takes the services they have become accustomed to in the name of more war? Let's hope not. Either way, this will serve to weaken the power and influence of the State.

As the existing government's economic power and support wither away, it will be more difficult for them to hire enforcers to follow their arbitrary orders, and formerly proud law-abiding, tax-paying citizens will flock to the underground economy. As this process takes places, the tables will turn and there will be a shift of power between the free people and the governments. The state would no longer have the upper hand in terms of raw physical strength. The drones, tanks, and other machinery of death will no longer be affordable for tyrants now that their formerly compliant tax cattle began to leave the farm by withdrawing their support for the system. Likewise, the soldiers and police forces who support oppression and suppression of revolution will have to rethink following orders once the propaganda of the state is destroyed. In fact, even in today's political climate, the government is having increasing difficulty finding people to fly their drones and wear their badges. On January 4, 2015, Air Force Chief of Staff General Mark Welsh sent an internal memo to General Herbert "Hawk" Carlisle complaining about drone pilots quitting in record numbers. Welsh said he feared that this exodus could cripple drone "combat readiness" for years to come. Indeed, military and police forces are constantly lowering standards and raising wages in attempts to lure more people into their order following campaign. Considering this, imagine the impact that could be made if large numbers of people began rejecting the government's legitimacy and organizing to strangle its support system.

The outcomes of this strategy are real and can be seen throughout history. The counter-economy can and will overtake the state when enough people are participating. One of the most obvious and historical examples of this is seen in the fall of the Soviet Union, which was brought on by widespread smuggling, tax avoidance and other black market activity. The underground economy was a part of everyday life for most people living in the Soviet Union, as it was actually necessary for their survival in many cases. Eventually, the ever growing restrictions and rations on the people stimulated the growth of the counter economy, and people began to trade untaxed goods and services until the government was starved of resources and support. At the time, Berkeley economist Gerard Roland noted that in the Soviet Union, *the logic of the second economy tended over time to undermine the logic of the command system and to lead to expanding black markets.*

This observation was later confirmed by Vladimir G. Treml and Michael V. Alexeev in their study, *The Second Economy and the Destabilization Effect of Its Growth on the State Economy in the Soviet Union: 1965-1989.* The study found that the disparity between legal income and legal spending grew significantly in the period between 1965 and 1989, meaning that people were spending much more money than they were making on the books, pointing to widespread black market activity. In their study, Treml and Alexeev conclude that the counter economy was largely responsible for the fall of the Soviet Union.

This was done entirely by accident, simply for the sake of survival, and even under these conditions the existing government collapsed. However, without the philosophy of agorism, anarchism or even libertarianism to follow through on this accomplishment, the oppressed people of the Soviet Union allowed a new government to be formed, and fell into bondage yet again. The collapse of the Soviet Union shows us that the counter-economy can be used to weaken, or even overthrow very powerful governments, but this victory will be short lived if people fail to follow through and apply the philosophy of agorism to their counter-economic activity.

When the state does get to a weakened point, fighting back against its agents becomes easier, and it becomes possible to physically push them back out of territories claimed by the agora. This dynamic can be seen in many developing countries where the central governments are very weak. When a protest or uprising happens in a place like this it is not unusual to see heavily armed and equipped government agents retreat from mobs of protesters that greatly outnumber them. This is not something that is possible in the U.S. today, but it is something that could be possible once the counter-economy takes enough power away from the State.

Still, we must remember that our goal is not to initiate violence against the State. Our goal is not a violent revolution, or revolution at all. The word implies revolving and going in circles, which is exactly what we should expect should we initiate force. As Samuel Konkin commented in *the New Libertarian Manifesto*, *"never initiate any act of violence regardless how likely a "libertarian" result may appear. To do so is to reduce yourself to a statist. There are no exceptions to this rule. Either you are fundamentally consistent or not."*

We want to abolish the state and create a world free of oppression and suffering, but we must not lose sight of ourselves in the pursuit of this goal. Every revolutionary throughout history who chose violence ended up becoming a monster and a shadow of what they pursued. Remain heart centered no matter how violent the state becomes or how divisive the

106

political climate. We are after an evolution of hearts and minds. To sustain a long term evolution (whether a physical fight against oppressors or a battle of hearts and minds) we must cultivate physical, mental, and spiritual strength and awareness. We believe the ideas presented in this series are a handbook which can be helpful in leading one down the path to freedom and autonomy. Finally, we are not claiming to be enlightened masters speaking of peace yet failing to embody the principles. Both of us have made plenty of mistakes and have much room to grow. However, we believe the principles and lifestyle espoused within our books are ideals to strive for. The Conscious Resistance offers the quickest way to lead our world towards a more free, ethical, and spiritually empowered world.

About the Authors - Derrick Broze

The last two books have recounted my activist path from 2010 until the present day. That story has been told before (and will be retold in detail in my next book) so I will not repeat what has been said twice before, other than to acknowledge that as of 2017 I am still involved with The Houston Free Thinkers activist community, The Conscious Resistance Network, and writing for Activist Post, The Anti Media, and Mint Press News. I plan to continue to write books on spiritual revelation and a fiction novel which illustrates the ideas presented within The Conscious Resistance trilogy. In the meantime I will be traveling the United States (2017) and Europe (2018) to spread the message of Holistic Anarchism.

About the Authors – John Vibes

John Vibes is an author and researcher who organizes a number of large events including the Free Your Mind Conference. He also has a publishing company where he offers a censorship free platform for both fiction and non-fiction writers. John is currently battling cancer naturally, without any chemo or radiation, and will be working to help others through his experience. Please check our other books for his full biography.

Acknowledgements

We would like to thank everyone who has supported our activism, journalism, and books. These essays are written with the intention of inspiring people to change the world by changing themselves. Whether or not this goal is achievable depends on how the individual readers integrate the information presented. If we were successful with this intention then we expect to see a growth of conscious, anti-statists in the coming decades. This book is written for those who are ready to change and those who are going to be born into a more free world. Thank you.

Suggested Reading List

We would like to offer a "Recommended Reading" list for those interested in further study of the material which has influenced our thinking. The list contains books covering politics, philosophy, psychology, and spirituality. We believe each of these areas of research are valuable for the holistic anarchist perspective.

New Libertarian Manifesto - Samuel Konkin III

An Agorist Primer - Samuel Konkin III

The Last Whole Introduction to Agorism - Samuel Konkin III

Agorist Class Theory - Samuel Konkin III & Wally Conger

Men Against the State - James J Martin

The Art of Not Being Governed - James C Scott

Society Against the State - Pierre Clastres

On Disobedience – Erich Fromm

The Other Path - Hermando De Soto

Neighborhood Power - Karl Hess

Community Technology - Karl Hess

Stealth of Nations - Robert Neuwirth

Human Action – Ludwig Von Mises

For a New Liberty – Murray Rothbard

A Beautiful Anarchy – Jeffrey Tucker

Markets Not Capitalism – Edited by Gary Chartier and Charles W. Johnson

Mutual Aid - Peter Kropotkin

No Treason: The Constitution of No Authority – Lysander Spooner

The Individualist Anarchists: An Anthology of Liberty - Frank H. Brooks

Rule By Secrecy – Jim Marrs

The Deep State – Michael Lofgren

Dark Alliance – Gary Webb

The Devils Chessboard – David Talbot

Tragedy & Hope – Carroll Quigley

The Terror Conspiracy – Jim Marrs

Spirit and Resistance – George Tinker

Non-Violent Communication – Marshall Rosenberg

The Four Agreements - Don Miguel Ruiz

The Untethered Soul – Michael A Singer

Black Elk Speaks - James G Neihardt

The Cosmic Serpent - Jeremy Narby

Science Set Free – Rupert Sheldrake

Narconomics – Tom Wainwright

The Underground History of American Education – John Taylor Gatto

Dumbing us Down – John Taylor Gatto

Sailboat Dairies – Michael Fielding

This book is dedicated to Samuel Konkin III and Karl Hess

(Samuel Konkin III)

(Karl Hess)

To find out more about The Conscious Resistance and Brain Paper Publishing, or to order more books please visit the following websites:

www.theconsciousresistance.com

www.brainpaperpublishing.com